品职教育·CFA 一考而过系列

CFA三级
知识框架图

何旋 李斯克 编著

机械工业出版社
China Machine Press

图书在版编目（CIP）数据

CFA 三级知识框架图 / 何旋，李斯克编著 . —北京：机械工业出版社，2018.5
（品职教育 · CFA 一考而过系列）

ISBN 978-7-111-59947-0

I. C… II. ①何… ②李… III. 金融 - 分析 - 资格考试 - 自学参考资料 IV. F83

中国版本图书馆 CIP 数据核字（2018）第 085618 号

作者根据 CFA 考试大纲，系统地梳理了 CFA 三级考试的知识框架和知识点，帮助所有考生迅速掌握 CFA 三级知识体系与结构。结合相关书籍，学生将在较短的时间内理清思路、掌握全局和要点，事半功倍。本书可助考生顺利通过考试。

CFA 三级知识框架图

出版发行：机械工业出版社（北京市西城区百万庄大街 22 号 邮政编码：100037）

责任编辑：杜若佳　　责任校对：李秋荣

印　　刷：北京文昌阁彩色印刷有限责任公司　　版　　次：2018 年 6 月第 1 版第 1 次印刷

开　　本：260mm × 185mm 1/16　　印　　张：15.75

书　　号：ISBN 978-7-111-59947-0　　定　　价：80.00 元

凡购本书，如有缺页、倒页、脱页，由本社发行部调换

客服热线：（010）68995261 88361066　　投稿热线：（010）88379007

购书热线：（010）68326294 88379649 68995259　　读者信箱：hzjg@hzbook.com

前 言

作为 CFA 培训师这么多年，最大的感触就是把单个知识点讲明白不难，帮助学生在头脑中建立起知识框架才最难。

书本由于展现形式的限制，只能通过线性的方式传递信息，但是知识点之间往往彼此关联，形成一个错综复杂的“知识网”。如果只能零散地学习这些知识点，没能建立起逻辑结构，既容易遗忘，又很难应用。

我们备课的过程，就是把这些线性的、无序的知识整理成有逻辑的知识框架，然后讲给学生。虽然会花大量的时间准备，但是培训效果很好，听了我们讲课的同学往往更容易高分通过考试。

我们自己备课整理出来的框架都要花费大量的时间，对于忙着为未来打拼的 CFA 考生来说，要自己花时间整理知识结构是不现实的。

于是，从 2013 年起，我们就试着把我们总结的逻辑结构，用知识框架图的形式画出来，并在我们的公众号“李老师与何老师的 CFA 学习课堂”上发布出来。没想到一下子吸引了大量的关注，平时去图书馆看书、考试时的考场外，都能看到很多人在翻阅我们发布的框架图，这让我们非常有成就感。

于是，我们每年都花大量的时间来完善我们的框架图，内容越来越丰富，框架越来越清晰，排版也越来越美观。

现在，这本框架图有机会正式出版，成为“品职教育 · CFA 一考而过系列”参考书中的一员，从复习资料变成正式出版物，也是对我们多年努力的一次肯定。

知识框架图的主要出发点是建立知识框架，所以内容是以结构及结论为主的，并没有知识点论述的过程。所以，知识框架图更适合作为配套参考书使用，CFA 三级的考生可以配套使用协会官方的教材，学完一个学科后配套地学习对应的知识框架图，可以在理解知识点的基础之上快速建立起逻辑结构。之后再配合做题来检验知识掌握情况，这应该是最高效的备考方法。

CFA 三级考试相比前两个级别，考生需要花费更多精力应对上午题的考核，而攻克上午题的重点，就在于知识框架的掌握。希望我们的总结可以帮各位考生节省整理知识点的时间，让备考 CFA 的道路更加平坦。祝各位备战 CFA 的考生们，都能达成各自的目标，成为更好的自己。

目 录

第 1 章

Ethics & Professional Standards

Standards
Professionalism
Knowledge of the law
Independence and objectivity
Misrepresentation
Misconduct
Integrity of capital markets
Material nonpublic information
Market manipulation
Duty to clients
Loyalty， prudence and care
Fair dealing
Suitability
Performance presentation
Preservation of confidentiality
Duty to employers
Loyalty
Additional compensation arrangements
Responsibility of supervisors
Investment
Diligence and reasonable basis
Communication with clients
Record retention
Conflicts of interest
Disclosure of conflicts
Priority of transaction
Referral fees
Responsibility as members
Conduct as members and candidates
Reference to CFA institute, designation

I (A) Knowledge of Law

<table>
<tr><td rowspan="1">条款要点</td><td>知法 → 守法 → 发现违法现象应该怎么做
1. 知法：不要成为法律专家 (not expert on compliance)，must comply with law directly governing（和你本职工作相关的法律法规）
2. 守法：Most strict (law or CFA institute standards)
3. 发现违法
（1）确切知道
● 原则：Dissociate，no requirement to report violations to governmental authorities
● 正确顺序：Report 给 supervisor 或 compliance department → 如果他们不处理，再 dissociate，即使辞职也在所不惜
（2）怀疑：Consult，but can't be absolved from requirements to compliance</td></tr>
<tr><td rowspan="2">案例总结</td><td>1. Members and candidates will need to be aware of the differences between cultural and religious laws（文化方面的惯例也要遵守）</td></tr>
<tr><td>2. Comply with the new guidance and regulation governing use of social media</td></tr>
</table>

注意：
1. 红色字体代表第 11 版 handbook 新增的比较重要的内容
2. 案例总结是把 case 当中容易判断错的结论摘录了下来，简单或者常规案例没有列出

I (B) Independence and Objectivity

条款要点	1. Gift （1）Best Practice：Reject gift that could be expected to compromise independence and objectivity （2）Gift from subject company (to research)：拒绝奢侈礼物，modest and normal gift is OK （3）Gift from client (to asset manager)：Client's gift should be disclosed，if not →violate I (B) IV (B)；disclose，但没有得到雇主同意 →violate IV (B)，不违反 I (B) [只要 disclose，就不违反 I (B)] 2. 各种关系 （1）Buy-Side clients：Institutional clients，portfolio managers 会对 sell side analyst 造成压力 （2）Fund manager relationships and Custodial Relationships：Hiring and retaining outside managers and third-party custodians 要独立客观 （3）Investment banking：Research analyst 不能受到投行的影响 （4）Performance Measurement and Attribution：作为 performance analysts，要披露基金经理是否有 stray from their mandate，alter the construction of composite 的现象，performance analyst 的独立客观性可能会受到基金经理和 sales 的影响 （5）Public companies：Analyst must not promise favorable report about the firm （6）Credit rating agency opinions：评级机构也要保持自己的独立客观性 （7）Influence during the Manager Selection：不能贿赂别人，也不能收受贿赂 （8）Issuer-Paid research：只能收 flat fee，和结论有关的任何 bonus 都不能收 （9）Travel Funding：最好自己付钱，可以接受一个 modestly arranged travel
案例总结	1. As credit analyst，must refuse to push the problematic bond to clients 2. Tickets to World Cup 属于比较奢侈的礼物 3. Travel Expense from External Manager：Should avoid the trip experience to impede his independence and objectivity in selection of managers

I (C) Misrepresentation

条款要点	1. 常规性的禁止吹牛 ● A company is prohibited from saying " we can provide all services you need". Proper way is to provide a list of services available ● Not misrepresent qualifications or services ● 禁止 guarantee the investment performance of volatile investment，但是如果本身 return 是可以保证的，也可以 guarantee 2. Omissions ● 使用 models and technical analysis 时，不能把 expected result 说成 fact ● 展示业绩时 prevent cherry picking (cherry picking 指挑一个好的披露) 3. Performance Reporting：可以没有 benchmark (比如 hedge fund)，但是如果有，benchmarks 要跟投资风格相匹配 4. Plagiarism 5. Using third-party information：必须要 disclose
案例总结	1. Typographical error 不属于，但是要及时改正 2. Use somebody's report，change a few words，sign your name，and get it out → 剽窃 3. P/E ratio，standard deviation → 用自己的语言总结，可以没有引用；若直接 copy，要有引用 4. Learns from a media → 先 verify，再引用原著 5. Unless the returns of a single fund reflect the performance of a firm as a whole，the use of a singular fund for performance comparisons should be avoided

I (D) Misconduct

条款要点	1. Lying，cheating，stealing，or other dishonest conduct 2. Negatively affects ability to perform professional activities（和本职工作相关的，个人信仰不属于违反）
案例总结	1. Personal bankruptcy：不违反 I (D)，但如果破产是因为 fraudulent or deceitful business conduct，那么就违反 I (D) 2. Intoxicated after lunch：影响正常工作，违反 I (D) 3. Environmental activist，破坏 petrochemical plant，不违反 I (D)

II (A) Material Nonpublic Information

<table>
<tr><td>条款要点</td><td>1. 原则：Trading or inducing others to trade on material nonpublic information →violate II (A)
2. MNI？
（1）Reliable source
（2）Clear impact
● Company-related information：Earnings，M&A，changes in assets，innovations，new licenses，developments regarding customers or suppliers，changes in management，auditor notification，events，legal disputes
● Macro-economy
● Large orders
● Well known analyst
● Qualified personnel
（3）Non-public：Selective disclosure may violate MNI（这种信息不算是 public，不能使用）
3. Mosaic Theory：Material public and nonmaterial nonpublic information → 不违反 II (A)
4. Using Industry Experts：要管理好从行业专家那里获得的 MNI，自己不能用，也不能给别人用</td></tr>
<tr><td>案例总结</td><td>1. Selective Disclosure：In a meeting with the finance director of the manufacturer and the other 10 largest shareholders of that company → 只是这几个人知道，属于选择性披露，还是 nonpublic
2. 从高管那里获得了 MNI，虽然质疑信息的可靠性，但是仍然买了这只股票 → 违反 II (A) [只要有 MNI，并且进行了交易，就违反 II (A)，不管有什么理由推脱]</td></tr>
</table>

II (B) Market Manipulation

条款要点	1. Info-based：Dissemination of false or misleading information 2. Transaction-based：Artificially affect prices or volume to give misleading impression of price movement 3. 不违反 II (B) 的 ● To increase liquidity，futures exchange insure the minimum trading volume ● Not prohibit trading strategies that exploit a diff in market power，info ● Not prohibit trade for tax purposes，selling then buying back
案例总结	Buy and sell the stock using the multiple accounts to raise the trading volume →violate II (B)

III (A) Loyalty, Prudence and Care

条款要点	1. Identify Client → 特殊的 ● Beneficiary：主要体现在 pension plans or trusts ● Mandate：主要体现在 mutual fund 2. Soft Dollar ● 要为客户 seek "best price" and "best execution" ● Soft dollar 要直接有利于 investment manager 帮助客户做投资决策。Whenever using client brokerage to purchase goods or services that do not benefit the client，should disclose to clients the methods or policies followed in addressing the potential conflict 3. Proxy Voting Policies ● 要做出有利于客户的投票 ● Voting proxies may not be necessary in all instances，要做 cost-benefit 分析 ● Members and candidates should disclose to clients their proxy voting policies 4. Understanding the Application of Loyalty，Prudence and Care ● Fiduciary duty：主要是 investment manager 和 advisor ● Standard III (A) does not render all members and candidates fiduciaries. Trade execution professional 没有 fiduciary duty，但是 trader 也必须要 use their skills and diligence to execute trades in the most favorable terms for clients
案例总结	1. Investment manager did not obtain the best execution for clients and indirectly used clients' brokerage to cover overhead expense，it is clear violation 2. Responsibility of asset manager of mutual fund is to manage the fund according to the investment policy statement of the fund. His actions should not be influenced by the needs of any particular fund investor

III (B) Fair Dealing

条款要点	1. Fairly ≠ equally；premium level service is okay，if not disadvantage or negatively affect other clients. Should be disclosed to clients and available to everyone 2. Trade：Equitable system，pro rata on order size，not on account size（为了能够买到相应份额，可以取整） 3. Analyst's Recommendation ● 第一时间发给所有客户 ● Material changes in prior recommendations should be communicated to all current clients ● Clients who do not know the changed recommendation and who place orders contrary to a current recommendation should be advised of the changed recommendation
案例总结	1. Weng uses email to issue a new recommendation to all his clients and then calls his 3 biggest clients to discuss the recommendation in detail → not violate 2. Burdette has violated Standard III (B) by sending an investment recommendation to a select group (只发给了 Twitter follower) of contacts prior to distributing it to all clients → violate 3. The recommended reports of helping the firm conduct after-the-fact reviews of how effectively the firm's advisers are dealing with their client's portfolios → not violate

III (C) Suitability

条款要点	了解客户 → 写 IPS → 要完全依据 IPS 来投资 1. Updating the IPS should be repeated at least annually and also prior to material changes 2. Diversification：是否适合客户要站在 portfolio 的角度，不能只看这个资产本身（主要是 derivatives，衍生品虽然风险高，但是还有风险对冲的作用） 3. Managing to an Index or Mandate：consistent with the stated mandate 4. Addressing Unsolicited Trade Requests：unsolicited trade 指的是和 IPS 不一致，但是客户自己要求做的 trade → 原则：the member or candidate should refrain from making the trade until he or she discusses the concerns with the client
案例总结	1. Covered call options in the equity portfolio → 风险对冲的作用，不违反 III (C) 2. High-income mutual fund，buys zero-dividend stock → 违反，因为不符合 fund 的投资风格 3. When selecting an external or sub-adviser，candidate needs to ensure that the new manager's services are appropriate for his clients

III (D) Performance Presentation

条款要点	1. Not misrepresent past performance or reasonably expected performance ● Not state or imply to obtain what was achieved in the past 2. Include terminated portfolio as part of performance history 3. The performance of weighted rate of return rather than a single performance 4. If the presentation is brief，must make available to clients and prospects，on request，the detailed information 5. Apply GIPS standards：这是 recommended，不是必需的，但是如果宣称遵守但实际没有遵守，就违反 III (D) 6. Full disclosure ：Whether simulated，when the performance record is that of a prior entity，whether gross of fees，net of fees，or after tax ● 模拟的业绩可以包含在业绩中，但是必须要 disclose
案例总结	1. The standard does not prohibit showing past record so long as it is fully disclosed where the performance comes from and the person's role in it 2. Modifying the performance attribution methodology without proper notifications to clients would fail to meet the requirements of Standard III (D) ● 如果 candidate 真的认为新的模型对于 performance attribution 更好 → 正确做法：He would need to report the results of both calculations to the client. The report should also include the reasons why the new methodology is preferred，which allow the client to make a meaningful comparison to prior results and provide a basis for comparing future attributions 3. Full information is provided when clients have sufficient information to judge the performance generated by the firm

III (E) Preservation of Confidentiality

条款要点	1. Must keep information about current，former，and prospective clients confidential unless ● The information concerns illegal activities on the part of the client ● Disclosure is required by law；or the client or prospective client permits disclosure of the information 2. If applicable law requires maintaining confidentiality，even if the information concerns illegal activities on the part of the client，should not disclose 3. Must continue to maintain the confidentiality of client records even after the client relationship has ended
案例总结	使用 social media ● Under the direction of her firm's technology and compliance departments，she established a new group page on an existing social media platform specifically for her clients →✓ ● The instructions also advised clients that all comments posted would be available to the public and thus the platform was not an appropriate method for communicating personal or confidential information →✓

IV (A) Loyalty to Employers

条款要点	Core rule：Whether injure the firm，deprive the firm of its profit，or compromise the advantage of employee's skill and capability 1. 在职时 ● Independent Practice：即 competitive business。Should not render services until they receive consent from their employer to all of the terms of the arrangement ● 可以在下班时间做兼职(非 competitive business)，只要不影响正常工作即可 ● 自己开公司：可以在下班时间做跟新公司注册相关的事务，但如果业务是跟现在雇主相竞争，离职前就不可以正式开展业务 2. Leaving an Employer （1）Before leaving，the following will cause a violation： ● Misappropriation of trade secrets ● Misappropriation of client lists. Memorizing client lists (name/address) is not permitted ● Misuse of confidential information ● Soliciting employer's clients prior to cessation of employment （2）After leaving，the following will cause a violation： ● Violation of terms in existing non-compete contract ● 只能带走 the skills and experience that an employee obtained ● Simple knowledge of names and existence of clients is not confidential information。可以通过 public information (比如网络) 找到客户 ● Firm records or research (即使是自己写的) should be erased or returned to employer 3. Use of Social Media：should adhere to the employer's policies and procedures ● **原则**：Placed her employer's interests ahead of her own personal interests

IV (A) Loyalty to Employers（续）

案例总结	1. 和雇主是 part time working agreement → 也要遵守 IV (A) 2. It is not a violation as long as candidate only prepares her new business on her own time outside the office 3. 业余时间的兼职是 mayor，如果兼职是 so extensive and time consuming 影响了正常工作，也是违反 4. Whistleblowing 不违反 IV (A) 5. Candidate is in violation of Standard IV (A) for disclosing confidential firm information through his personal blog. The recommendations on the firm's blog to clients are not freely available across the internet，but his blog provides the firm's recommendation. Additionally，by posting research commentary on his personal blog，Gupta is using firm resources for his personal advantage. To comply with Standard IV (A) members and candidates must receive consent from their employer prior to using company resources

IV (B) Additional Compensation Arrangements

条款要点	No gifts，benefits，compensation or consideration are to be accepted which may create a conflict of interest with the employer's interest unless written consent is received from all parties 注意：只有跟本职工作相关的，可能会 create a conflict of interest 的，才是 additional compensation
案例总结	1. 客户给的 trip to Monaco →disclose，并且收到雇主 written consent 才能收 2. 目标公司给的 non-monetary benefits →disclose，并且收到雇主 written consent 才能收

IV (C) Responsibility of Supervisors

<table>
<tr><td>条款要点</td><td>1. 预防 → 发现 → 下属违反如何行动?
（1）积极预防和发现
● Establishing policies and procedures to achieve compliance with the code and applicable law，and reviewing employee actions to determine whether they are following the rules
● Members and candidates should implement education and training programs
● Establishing incentives—monetary or otherwise—for employees not only to meet business goals but also to reward ethical behavior
（2）下属违反
● Should take steps to ensure that the violation will not be repeated，by placing limits on the employee's activities or increasing the monitoring of the employee's activities
2. Can delegate，but not relieve of supervisory responsibility</td></tr>
<tr><td>案例总结</td><td>1. Candidate Violated Standard IV (C) by not exercising reasonable supervision when he agrees to send out the memo without reasonable and adequate basis
2. Members and candidates should ensure that their firm has appropriate policies and procedures in place to detect inappropriate actions
3. Supervisor should establish reasonable procedures to prevent the unauthorized dissemination of company research through social media networks</td></tr>
</table>

V (A) Diligence and Reasonable Basis

条款要点	基本原则：Have a reasonable and adequate basis，supported by appropriate research and investigation，for any investment analysis，recommendation，or action 1. Using Secondary or Third-Party Research： ● Make reasonable and diligent efforts to determine whether it is sound ● 如果发现第三方研究报告确实好，当成自己的发给客户 → 违反 I (C)，剽窃 2. Using Quantitatively Oriented Research： ● Candidates are not required to become experts in every technical aspect of the models，they must understand the assumptions and limitations inherent in any model ● Candidates should make reasonable efforts to test the output 3. Developing Quantitatively Oriented Techniques：Higher level of diligence ● A thorough testing of the model and resulting analysis should be completed prior to product distribution ● Members and candidates need to consider the source and time horizon of the data used as inputs in financial models 4. Group Research ：If the consensus opinion has a reasonable and adequate basis and is independent and objective，可以在团体报告上签名
案例总结	1. Always recommend "hot" issue indicates NO reasonable basis 2. The selection of an external adviser or sub-adviser should be based on a full and complete review of the advisers' services，performance history，and cost structure 3. Analysis of an investment that results in a reasonable basis for recommendation does not guarantee that the investment will have no down-side risk（即使审慎分析和研究，结果仍然可能有损失）

V (B) Communication with Clients

条款要点	1. Disclose to clients and prospective clients the basic format and general principles of the investment processes ● If recommendations are in capsule form (such as a recommended stock list), should notify clients that additional information and analyses are available upon request 2. Must promptly disclose any material changes that might materially affect those processes 3. Distinguish between fact and opinion in the presentation of investment analysis and recommendations 4. Identifying Risk and Limitations of Analysis ● Examples of such factors and attributes include but are not limited to investment liquidity and capacity
案例总结	1. Candidate should disclose a material error in the investment process 2. If significant limitations are complicated to grasp and clients do not have the technical background required to understand them, candidate should either educate the clients or ascertain whether the fund is suitable for each client

V (C) Record Retention

条款要点	1. Records may be maintained either in hard copy or electronic form ● If no regulatory guidance，CFA Institute recommends maintaining records for at least 7 years. If there is a legal requirement for retention period，follow the legal requirement 2. Records created in professional activities are the property of the firm. When leaving the firm，cannot take those records，including originals or copies of supporting records of his work，to the new employer without the express consent of the previous employer → 如果带走，既违反 IV (A)，又违反 V (C)。正确做法是：re-create the supporting records at the new firm
案例总结	The records created by candidate supporting the research model he developed at previous firm are the records of previous employer. He can't take the record without the permission

VI (A) Disclosure of Conflicts

<table>
<tr><td>条款要点</td><td>1. Make full and fair disclosure of all conflicts of interest (一般是针对 research 的角色)
● Corporate financing or market making relationship
● Security holding
● Directorship
● Individual relationship
2. 也可以将有 conflict of interest 的股票放在 restricted list 里面 (只陈述 fact，不表达自己的 opinion)
3. 只要违反 VI (A)，就违反 I (B)</td></tr>
<tr><td>案例总结</td><td>1. Conflict of interest 的表现：
● Candidate's colleagues sit on the board of directors of subject company's subsidiaries
● Subject company 是本公司的股东
● Candidate's wife inherits $3 million of subject company's stock
● Compensation arrangement that may create a conflict of interest
2. Candidate Violated Standard VI (A) by failing to disclose the additional compensation to his clients and employer，this conflict of interest would interfere his independence and objectivity → 也违反 IV (B) I (B)
3. Standard VI (A) would not require candidate to disclose her personal or retirement investments in large diversified mutual funds</td></tr>
</table>

VI (B) Priority of Transaction

条款要点	Client > employer > individual ● 这个条款主要强调的是不能 front running (先于客户而交易) ● Must have enough time to let clients have opportunities to respond to your recommendation
案例总结	1. Seven minutes after informed the sell recommendation for a stock in an in-house meeting，Riley closes out a long call option in that stock and establishes a sizable put position → Riley exploited the sell recommendation and did not give customers the opportunity to act before the firm itself did. It's a violation 2. Toffler has violated Standard VI (B) by breaching her duty to her parents by treating them differently from her other accounts simply because of the family relationship. As fee-paying clients of Esposito Investments，Toffler's parents are entitled to the same treatment as any other client of the firm → 也违反 III (B)

VI (C) Referral Fees

条款要点	Members and candidates must inform their employer，clients，and prospective clients of any benefit received for referrals of customers and clients
案例总结	1. A broker directs certain prospective accounts to a asset manager in exchange for research service and commission business. The asset manager must inform the client the referral fee payable in services and commissions to a broker 2. Handley works for the trust dept，and receives compensation for each referral he makes to brokerage dept，and the personal management dept. He must disclose the referral arrangement even within the firm 3. A portfolio manager for a bank，receives additional monetary compensation from his employer when he is successful in assisting in sales process. He must disclose → 如果不 disclose，违反 VI (C) 和 IV (B)

VII (A) Conduct as Members and Candidates

条款要点	1. 考场纪律 2. Improperly using an association with CFA Institute to further personal or professional goals，违反 VII (A) 3. Expressing opinions regarding the CFA Program or CFA Institute is OK
案例总结	1. By revealing portions covered on the exam and areas not covered， she did violate Standard VII (A) 2. She tells her clients that her Executive Committee membership will allow her to better assist her clients in keeping up with changes to the Standards and facilitating their compliance with the changes→ violate VII (A)

VII (B) Reference to CFA Institute，Designation

条款要点	1. Mustn't cite the expected date of exam completion and award of charter 2. A candidate who has passed level III but has not received charter can't use CFA designation 3. It's only appropriate to use CFA logo on the business card or letterhead of each individual CFA charterholder 4. The order of CFA and CPA doesn't matter 5. If a charterholder fails to meet membership requirements，he can't use CFA designation. Until membership is reactivated，can only state that they were charterholders in the past 6. If a candidate passes each level of the exam on the first try and wants to state that he or she did so，that is not a violation because it is a statement of fact，but must not over-promise the competency and future investment results
案例总结	1. Implying that (1) CFA charterholders achieve better investment results and (2) those who pass the exams on the first try are more successful would violate Standard VII (B) 2. The candidate has violated Standard VII (B) because his right to use the CFA designation was suspended when he failed to file his Professional Conduct Statement and stopped paying dues 3. The CFA Logo must not be incorporated in a company name 4. Must include the charterholder's full name along with any reference to the CFA designation

第 2 章

Behavioral Finance

Reading 5

THE BEHAVIORAL FINANCE PERSPECTIVE

Behavioral Finance vs. Traditional Finance

Framework

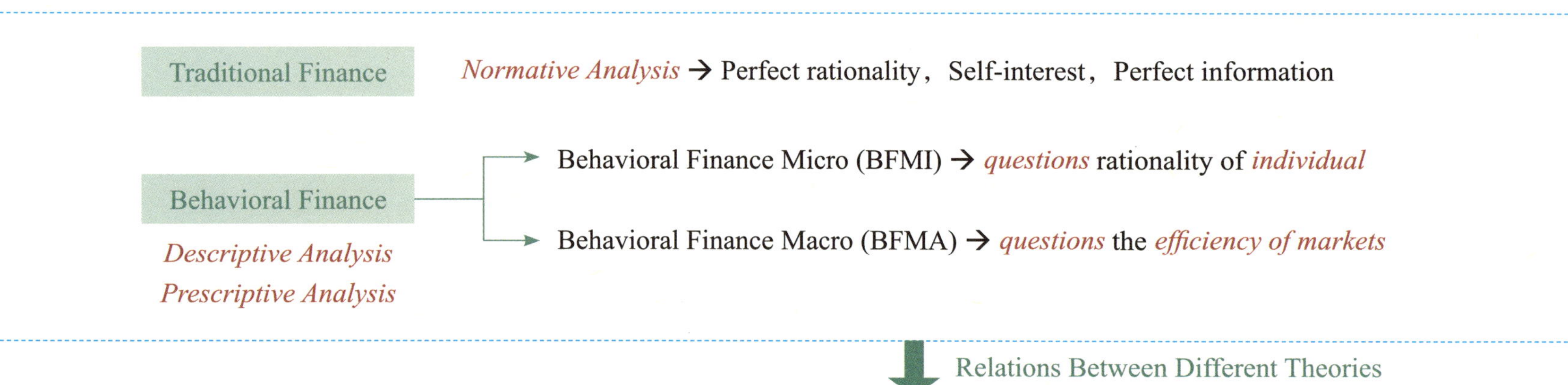

Relations Between Different Theories

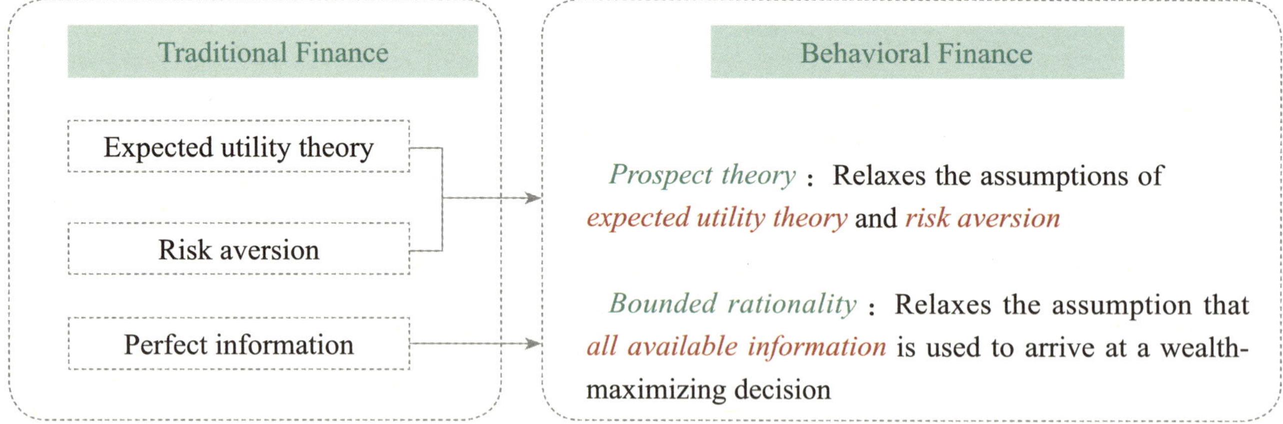

BFMI：Traditional Finance Theory

Expected Utility Theory

REM → Traditional

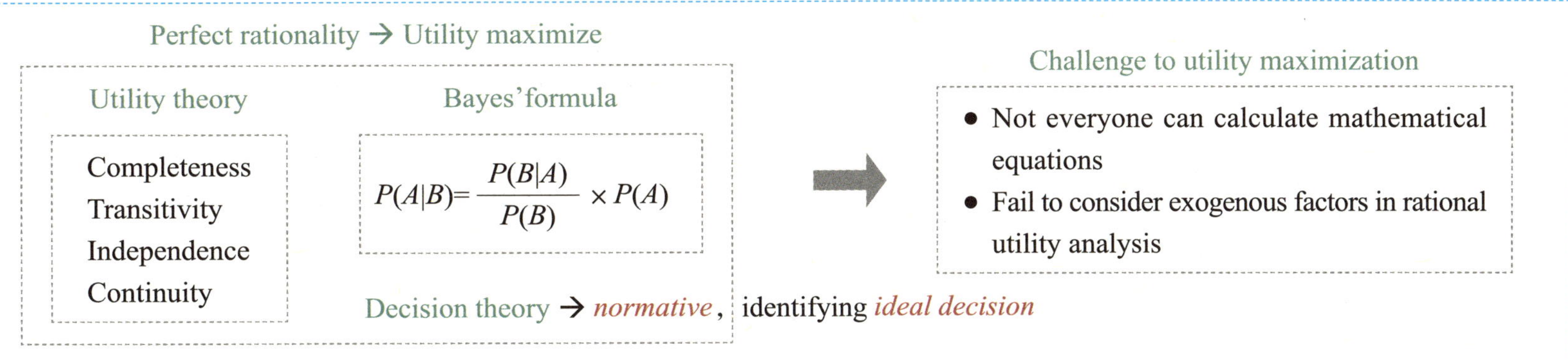

Risk Averse

Traditional

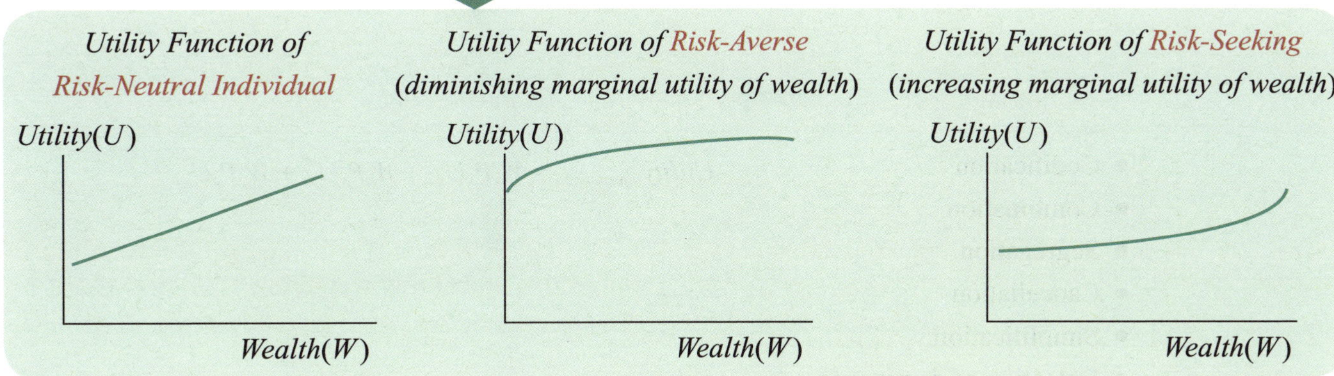

BFMI：Behavior Finance Theory

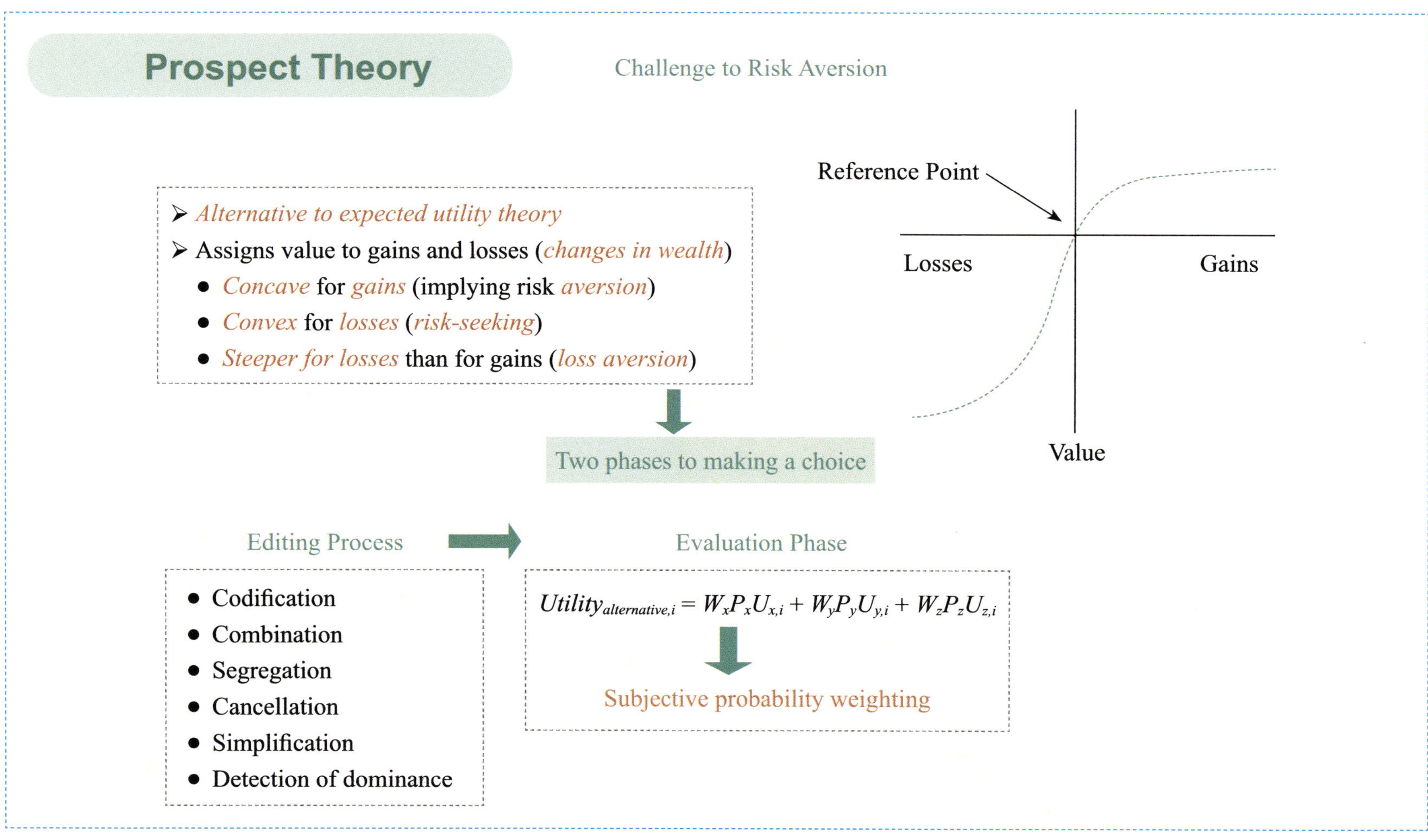

Bounded Rationality

- *Satisficing* is finding an *acceptable solution* as opposed to optimizing
- The *optimal solution* is the one that maximizes the utility *realizable from the situation*

Neuro-economics 概念

- *Support*: Understanding the brain activity of judgment and making choices
- *Critics*: Its effect on the economic theory remains to be seen

Traditional Finance Assumes	Bounded Rationality and Prospect Theory Assumes
Unlimited perfect knowledge	Capacity limitations on knowledge
Utility maximization	Satisfice
Fully rational decision making	Cognitive limits on decision making
Risk aversion	Reference dependence to determine gain or loss leading to possible cognitive errors

BFMA：Perspectives on Market Behavior

EMH

Traditional

Types	Assumption	Implication
Weak-Form EMH	Market info.	Technical Analysis ×
Semi Strong-Form EMH	Public info.	Fundamental Analysis ×
Strong-Form EMH	All info.	Nobody can win the market

Anomalies

- Size Effect
- Value Effect
- Moving Averages
- Trading Range Break
- January Effect

Portfolio Construction

Behavioral Finance

Consumption and Savings

- Framing
- Self-control
- Mental accounting

Framing

Current income, currently owned assets, or PV of future income

Behavioral Asset Pricing

- *The required return* = R_f + *fundamental risk premium* + *sentiment premium*

Behavioral Portfolio Theory

✓ Construct by *layers*

✓ *Asset number in a layer*

- Risk aversion
- Information advantage
- Loss-averse

Adaptive Markets Hypothesis

- *Revised version* of the *EMH*

Reading 6

THE BEHAVIORAL BIASES OF INDIVIDUALS

Cognitive Errors and Emotional Biases

Cognitive Errors	Emotional Biases
✓ *Cognitive errors* ● Belief perseverance biases ● Processing biases	✓ *Emotional biases*

Belief Perseverance Biases

可以纠正

Conservatism bias	People maintain their prior views or forecasts by inadequately incorporating new information
Confirmation bias	Individuals tend to notice only information that agrees with their perceptions or beliefs
Representativeness	People tend to classify new information based on past experiences and classifications
Illusion of control	People tend to believe that they can control or influence outcomes when， in fact， they cannot
Hindsight bias	People may see past events as having been predictable and reasonable to expect

Representativeness
- Base-Rate Neglect
- Sample-Size Neglect → *overweight the information in the small sample*

Processing Biases

Anchoring	People generally estimate a value by envisioning some initial default number
Mental accounting	People treat one sum of money differently from another equal-sized sum based on which mental account the money is assigned to *Goals-based investing* ★ →pyramid
Framing	A person answers a question differently based on the way in which it is asked
Availability bias	Estimating the probability of an outcome based on how easily the outcome comes to mind

Emotional Biases

Loss aversion	People tend to strongly prefer avoiding losses as opposed to achieving gains
Overconfidence	People demonstrate unwarranted faith in their intuitive reasoning，judgments，cognitive abilities ● 表现 Prediction overconfidence & Certainty overconfidence ● 原因：Self-attribution bias → self-enhancing bias & self-protecting bias
Self-control bias	Fail to act in pursuit of their long-term，overarching goals because of a lack of self-discipline
Status quo bias	An emotional bias in which people do nothing instead of making a change
Endowment bias	People value an asset more when they hold rights to it than when they do not
Regret-aversion bias	Avoid making decisions that will result in action out of fear that the decision will turn out poorly

Behaviorally Modified Asset Allocation

	Cognitive Bias	Emotional Bias
High wealth Low SLR	➢ Modest changes ➢ +/− 5% to 10% maximum per asset class	➢ Larger changes ➢ +/− 10% to 15% maximum per asset class
Low wealth High SLR	➢ Close to the rational asset allocation ➢ +/− 0 to 3% maximum per asset class	➢ Modest changes ➢ +/− 5% to 10% maximum per asset class

- Emotional bias 允许的偏离 >cognitive bias
- High wealth 允许偏离度 >low wealth
- High wealth 的 cognitive bias 允许偏离度 =low wealth 的 emotional bias

如何诊断客户行为偏差? Diagnostic Questions

Basic Diagnostic Questions for Behavioral Bias

Behavioral Bias	Diagnostic Question
Loss Aversion	Imagine you make an investment that drops 25% in the first six months. You are unsure if it will come back. What would you normally do?
Endowment	How would you describe your emotional attachment to possessions or investment holdings?
Status Quo	How would you describe the frequency of your trading?
Anchoring	You purchase a stock at $50 per share. It goes up to $60 in a few months，and then it drops to $40 a few months later. You are uncertain what will happen next. How would you respond?
Mental Accounting	Do you categorize your money by different financial goals，or look at the bigger financial picture?
Regret Aversion	Have you ever made an investment that you have regretted making? How did that affect your future investing decisions?
Hindsight	Do you believe investment outcomes are generally predictable or unpredictable?
Framing	Assume you have agreed to a financial plan created by your adviser that has a projected return of 9% and an annual standard deviation of +/−15% (a typical plan). Would it surprise you to know that statistically in the worst case，the plan's return could be negative 36% or more in one year out of 100? Would this information cause you to rethink your risk tolerance?
Conservatism	Assume you make an investment based on your own research. An adviser presents you with information that contradicts your belief about this investment. How would you respond?

Basic Diagnostic Questions for Behavioral Bias（续）

Behavioral Bias	Diagnostic Question
Availability	Do you ever make investment decisions (such as selecting a mutual fund or online broker) based on word-of-mouth or name recognition?
Representativeness	Have you ever made a new investment because of its apparent similarity to a past successful investment (e.g., a tech stock or value stock) without doing research to validate the new investment's merits?
Overconfidence	Suppose you make a winning investment. How do you generally attribute the success of your decision?
Confirmation	Suppose you make an investment based on your own research. The investment doesn't move up as much as you thought it might. How are you likely to respond?
Illusion of Control	You are offered two free lottery tickets. You may either select your own numbers or have a machine do it. What would you do?
Self-Control	Do you tend to save or spend disposable income?

Reading 7

BEHAVIORAL FINANCE AND INVESTMENT PROCESSES

Behavioral Finance and Investment Processes

Classifying Investors

- ✓ Barnewall two-way model
- ✓ BBK five-way model
- ✓ Pompain model

掌握投资者的特征，判断与这类投资者的沟通方法

Limitations of Classification

- ✓ Individuals exhibit *both cognitive and emotional biases*
- ✓ Individuals may exhibit *multiple investor types*
- ✓ Behavioral *changes as they age*
- ✓ Individuals *require unique treatment* even if classified as the *same investor type*
- ✓ Individuals act *irrationally* at *different times*

Excess Trading

掌握原因

- ✓ Overconfidence
- ✓ Self selection
- ✓ Disposition effect
- ✓ Home bias

DC Plan 中常见偏差

- ✓ Status quo bias
  - 克服方法：Target date funds
- ✓ Naive diversification/conditional naive diversification
- ✓ Concentration in employer stock
  - 原因：Familiarity/ overconfidence/ framing/ status quo/ loyalty effect

Investment Committees 常见偏差

偏差及克服方法

Analysts Forecast 偏差

✓ **Overconfidence**
- Illusion of knowledge bias
- Illusion of control bias
- Representativeness
- Availability bias
- Self-attribution bias
- Hindsight bias
- Sample size

✓ **The way management presents information**
- Framing
- Anchoring and adjustment
- Availability

✓ **Biased research**
- The confirmation bias
- Gambler's fallacy
- Representative bias

掌握原因

Market Anomalies 原因

Momentum effect

Herding
Availability bias
Fear of regret

Financial bubbles and crashes

Overconfidence
Confirmation bias
Self attribution bias
Hindsight bias
Regret aversion
Disposition effect

Value vs. growth - bias

Halo effect
Home bias

第3章

Private Wealth Management

Reading 8

MANAGING INDIVIDUAL INVESTOR PORTFOLIOS

Individual IPS

获取客户信息，
理解不同的客户特征

→

- Source of wealth → Entrepreneurial vs. inheritance activity
- Measure of wealth → 与 spending 对应
- Stage of life →
  - Foundation phase
  - Accumulation phase
  - Maintenance phase
  - Distribution phase

  理解不同阶段的客户特征

↓ 根据客户信息写 IPS
做最近 10 年的真题即可★★

Objective

Objective	考点
Return	计算 required return → After tax nominal & Pretax nominal return ★★ 两种形式 → 已知终值（close end）& 未知终值（open end）
Risk	✓ 考点 →Ability &willingness to take risk，判断 above or below average ★★ (follow the narrower of the two) ✓ 影响因子与 Ability 相关性★ ● Time horizon (ρ>0)，Portfolio size (ρ>0)，Goal importance (ρ<0)，Spending needs (ρ<0)，Flexibility (ρ>0) ✓ Willingness→ 看投资者行为及持仓情况

Constraints

Constraints	考点
Time Horizon ★★	考点 → 识别几个 stage，及每个 stage 起始时间。以重大 CF 改变为准
Tax Considerations	以文章中的 tax 描述为准 → 考的比较少，注意 low basis stock
Liquidity Needs ★★	求 liquidity needs 的大小 → 计算，短期 & 需要卖的资产变现部分，注意 cash reserve
Legal & Regulatory	Prudent investor rule → 考的少，以文章描述为准，
Unique Circumstances	以文章描述为准，如 donation 等 → donation 增加 flexibility，增加 ability to take risk

根据 IPS 选组合　　以上过程为静态规划过程，应考虑未来变数

选适合的组合 → 排除法

- Fail to meet the after-tax return objective
- Violate shortfall statement
- Includes disallowed asset classes
- Fails to meet liquidity requirements
- Always minimize cash (3～6 months' living expense)
- 还有剩余可选组合，选择 Sharpe ratio 最大的

Monte Carlo Simulation ★

概念

优点：

- It more accurately portrays risk-return tradeoffs
- Can illustrate the tradeoffs between the attainment of short-term and long-term goals
- Provides more realistic modeling of taxes
- Better suited to assessing multi-period effects

缺点：

- Simplistic use of historical data
- Simulate the return of asset classes
- Tax modeling that is simplistic and not tailored

Reading 9

TAXES AND PRIVATE WEALTH MANAGEMENT IN A GLOBAL CONTEXT

Taxes and Private Wealth Management

Global Taxation Regimes

概念，了解

Regime	Ordinary Income Tax Structure	Favorable Treatment for Interest Income?	Favorable Treatment for Dividend Income?	Favorable Treatment for Capital Gains?
Common Progressive	Progressive	Yes	Yes	Yes
Heavy Dividend Tax	Progressive	Yes	No	Yes
Heavy Capital Gain Tax	Progressive	Yes	Yes	No
Heavy Interest Tax	Progressive	No	Yes	Yes
Light Capital Gain Tax	Progressive	No	No	Yes
Flat and Light	Flat	Yes	Yes	Yes
Flat and Heavy	Flat	Yes	No	No

Tax 计算★★

计算。要会计算 tax drag，% 及 $ 形式。注意是基于收益部分而不是总额进行计算 ★

税种	N 年后税后金额	Tax drag
Accrual taxes	$FVIF_{AT}=[\,1+R\,(1-T)\,]^N$	1. Tax drag% > tax rate 2. N ↑ or R ↑→tax drag $ & % ↑
Deferred capital gain tax	$FVIF_{CGT}=(1+R)^N-[\,(1+R)^N-1]\times T_{CG}$ $FVIF_{CGT,MV\neq Basis}=[(1+R)^N(1-T_{CG})\,]+T_{CG}-(1-B)T_{CG}$	1. Tax drag % = tax rate 2. N ↑ or R ↑→tax drag% 不变 3. N ↑ or R ↑→tax drag$↑
Wealth-based taxes	$FVIF_{WT}=[(1+R)(1-T_W)]^N$	1. Tax drag % > tax rate 2. N ↑→ tax drag % & $↑ 3. R ↑→tax drag % ↓ & $↑

Blend taxing environments

计算

1. 计算 N 年后税后金额

$$T_{ECG}=T_{CG}\left[\frac{1-(P_I+P_D+P_{CG})}{1-(P_IT_I+P_DT_D+P_{CG}T_{CG})}\right]$$

$$FVIF_T=[(1+R_{ART})^N(1-T_{ECG})+T_{ECG}-(1-B)T_{CG}]$$

$$R_{ART}=R(1-realized\ tax\ rate)=R[1-(P_IT_I+P_DT_D+P_{CG}T_{CG})]$$

2. 计算 effective annual return →$FV=PV(1+r)^N$

3. 计算 accrual equivalent tax rate →$R_{AE}=R(1-T_{AE})$

投资账户★★★

与 IPS 写作密切相关

Taxable accounts → 最常规投资账户，用个人扣除个人所得税后到手的金额进行投资，投资收益要交税

Tax-deferred accounts → 主要是 pension 账户，投资时免扣个人所得税，账户内投资收益免税，但是 withdraw 时就提取金额征税

$FVIF_{TDA}=(1+R)^N(1-T_N)$

Tax-exempt accounts → 个人扣除个人所得税后进行投资，投资收益及 withdraw 免税

$FVIF_{TEA}=(1-T_0)(1+R)^N$

额度有限，所以要做税务规划

Tax Alpha

掌握特征

Tax loss harvesting

HIFO

Reading 10

ESTATE PLANNING IN A GLOBAL CONTEXT

Estate Planning Basic Concepts

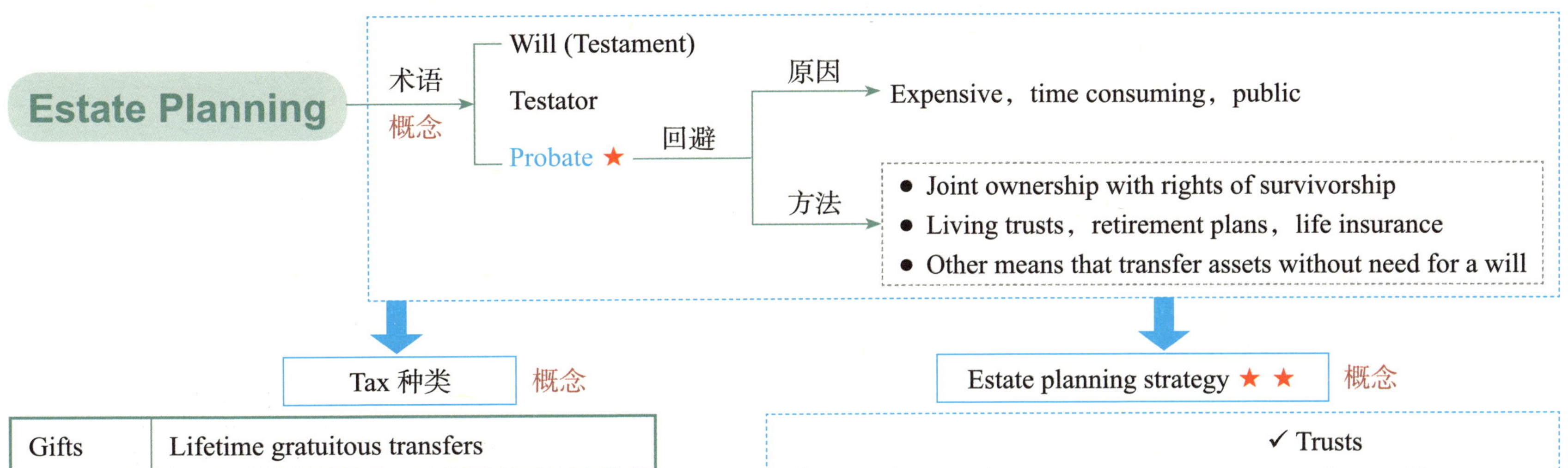

Gifts	Lifetime gratuitous transfers
Bequests	Testamentary transfers ● Estate taxes: paid by transferor ● Inheritance taxes: paid by recipient

Relief from double taxation ★，会计算

- *Credit method* → $T_{credit\ method} = Max[T_{residence},\ T_{source}]$
- *Exemption method* → $T_{exemption\ method} = T_{source}$
- *Deduction method* → $T_{deduction\ method} = T_{source} + T_{residence}(1 - T_{source})$

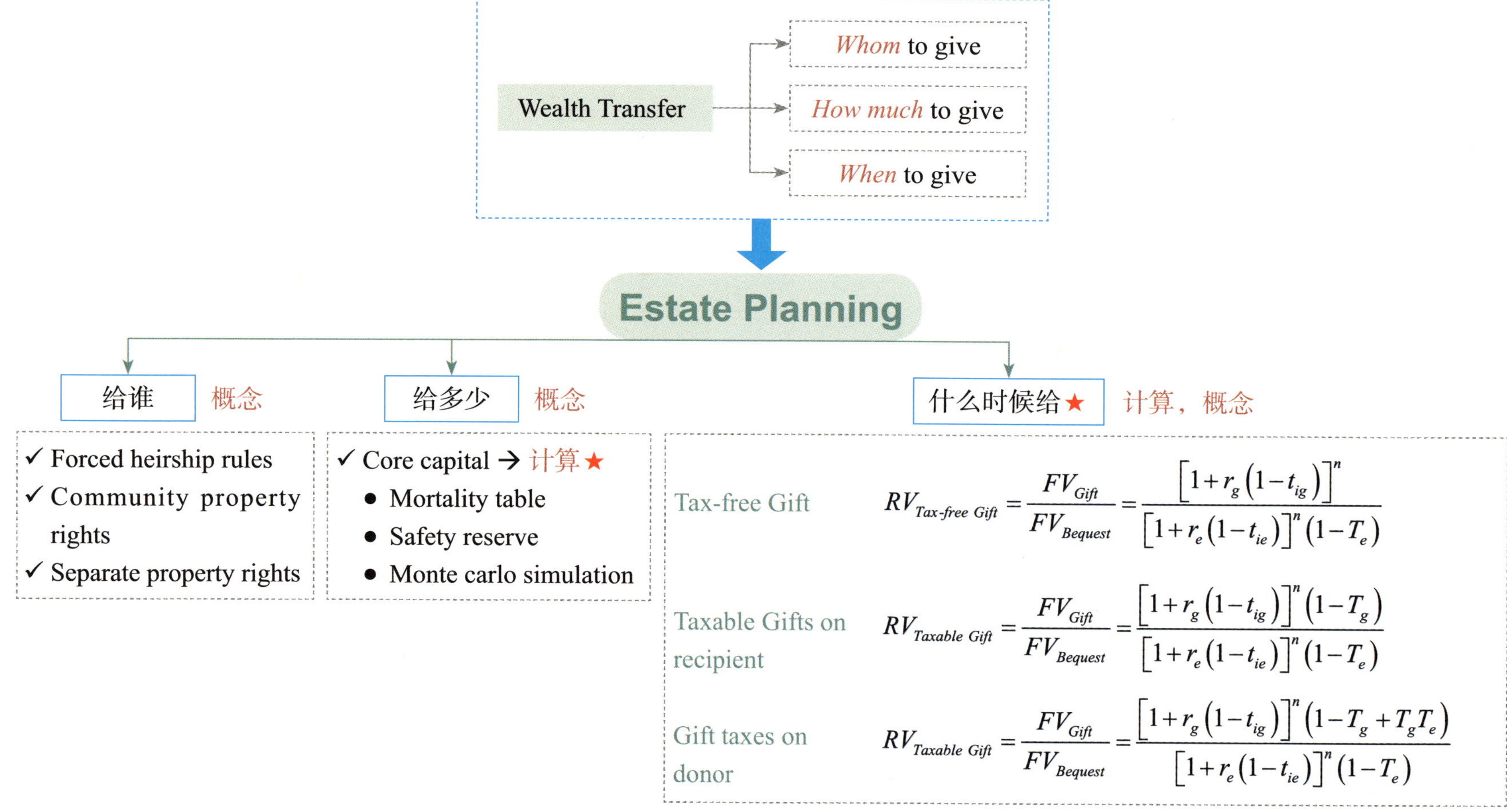
Wealth Transfer
Whom to give
How much to give
When to give
Estate Planning
给谁
概念
给多少
概念
什么时候给★
计算，概念
✓ Forced heirship rules
✓ Community property rights
✓ Separate property rights
✓ Core capital → 计算★
Mortality table
Safety reserve
Monte carlo simulation
Tax-free Gift
$RV_{Tax\text{-}free\ Gift}=\frac{FV_{Gift}}{FV_{Bequest}}=\frac{[1+r_g(1-t_{ig})]^n}{[1+r_e(1-t_{ie})]^n(1-T_e)}$
Taxable Gifts on recipient
$RV_{Taxable\ Gift}=\frac{FV_{Gift}}{FV_{Bequest}}=\frac{[1+r_g(1-t_{ig})]^n(1-T_g)}{[1+r_e(1-t_{ie})]^n(1-T_e)}$
Gift taxes on donor
$RV_{Taxable\ Gift}=\frac{FV_{Gift}}{FV_{Bequest}}=\frac{[1+r_g(1-t_{ig})]^n(1-T_g+T_gT_e)}{[1+r_e(1-t_{ie})]^n(1-T_e)}$

Reading 11

CONCENTRATED SINGLE-ASSET POSITIONS

Concentrated Single-Asset Positions

概念

Three Major Types

Publicly traded stock
A privately owned business
Real estate

Risk in Illiquid Assets

Systematic risk
Company-specific risk
Property-specific risk

Common Objectives

Reduced the risk
Generate liquidity
Optimize tax efficiency

难实现的原因

Affecting All Positions

Tax liability
Illiquidity and/or high transaction

Specific Objectives

Restrictions on sale
A desire for control
To create wealth
The asset may have other uses

Institutional and Capital Market Constraints

Margin lending rules
Securities law and regulations
Contractual restrictions and employer mandates
Capital market limitations

Psychological Consideration→ 克服方法

Goal-based Decision Process ★

Goal-based Decision Process ★ 

Primary Capital

Bucket	Contant
Personal risk bucket	Protect the client from *poverty or a drastic deadline* in lifestyle ● Low-risk assets ● Personal residence
Market risk bucket	*Maintain* the client's existing standard of living ● Stocks and bonds earning an expected market return
Aspirational risk bucket	High-risk investments could substantially *improve* the client's standard of living ● Positions in private business ● Concentrated stock holdings ● Real estate investments， and other riskier positions

Managing Risks of Concentrated Position

Managing Single-stock Positions

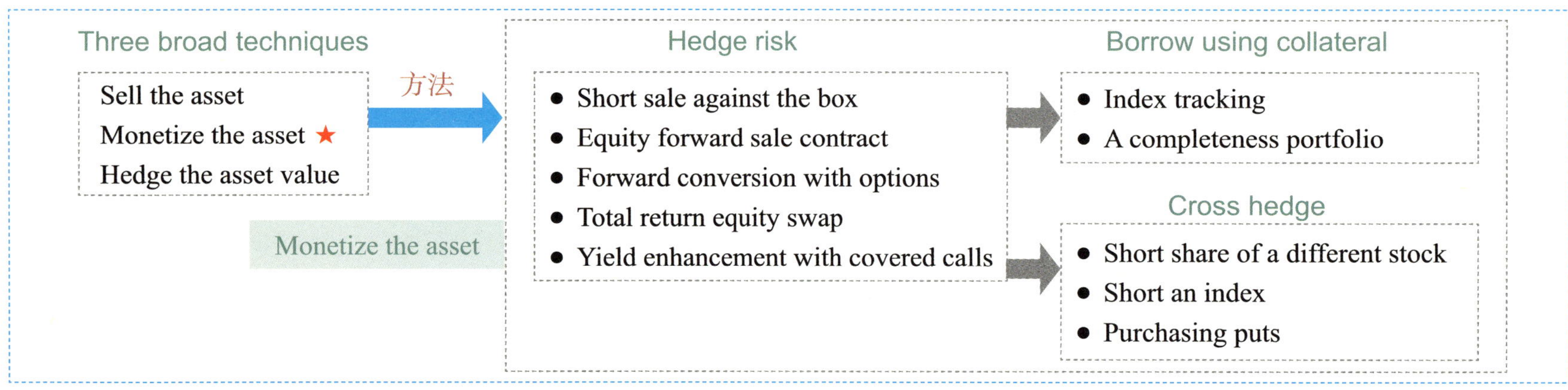

Managing Privately Owned Business

- Strategic buyers
- Private equity fund
- Recapitalization
- Sale to (other) management or key employees → 缺点

- Divestiture
- A sale or gift to family members
- A personal line of credit secured by company shares
- IPO
- ESOP

Managing Real Estate

- Mortgage financing
- Donor-advised fund or charitable trust
- Sale and leaseback

Reading 12

RISK MANAGEMENT FOR INDIVIDUALS

Risk Management for Individuals

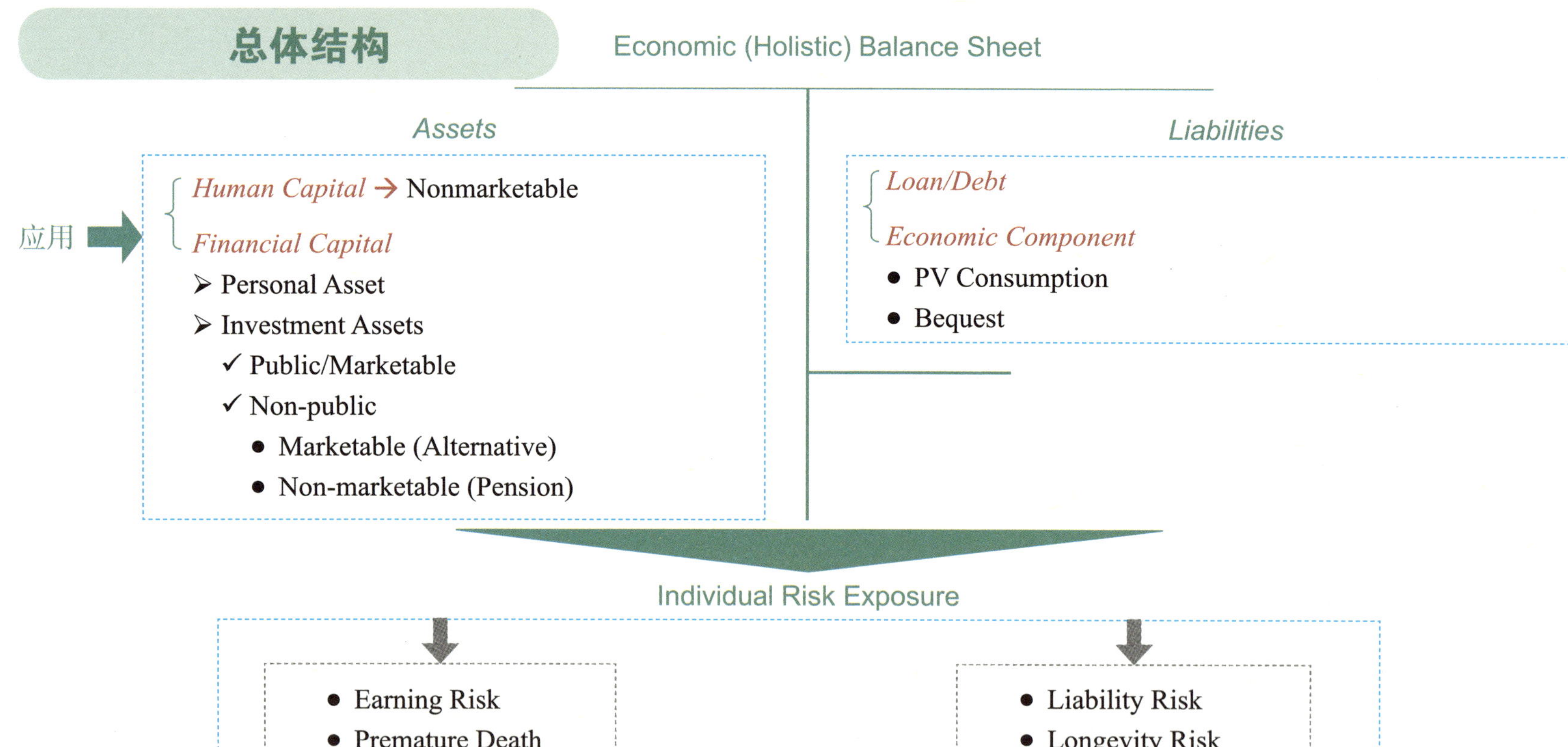

Traditional vs. Economic Balance Sheet

Traditional vs. Economic Balance Sheet

✓ A *traditional balance sheet* includes assets and liabilities that are generally relatively *easy* to *quantify*

✓ An *economic balance sheet* provides a useful overview of *total wealth portfolio* by supplementing

- Assets with *human capital* and *pension* wealth
- Including additional liabilities， such as *consumption* and *bequest goals*

Financial Stages of Life

✓ *Economic (Holistic) Balance Sheet*

- The *primary goal* is to *accurately depict* overall financial health
- Allows an individual to map out the *optimal level* of *future consumption* and *non-consumption goals* (such as *bequests* or other *transfers*)
- Younger households with greater human capital， in addition to *spending more to protect the value of this human capital* early in the life cycle， will be able to plan for more generous *retirement savings goals* than households with comparatively lower human capital

✓ Education phase
✓ Early career
✓ Career development
✓ Peak accumulation
✓ Pre-retirement
✓ Early retirement
✓ Late retirement

应用

$\rho(HC, FC)$ 越小越好

- Human capital
  - *Equity-like* → 投 *Bond*
  - *Fixed income-like* → 投 *Stock*
- Financial assets → 金融资产内部分散化也很重要

- 年轻 → *HC* 大
- 年老 → *FC* 大

Insurance

Basic Concept

Uses of Life Insurance

- Hedge risk of *premature death*
- *Estate-planning tool*
- Tax-sheltered instrument

Types of Life Insurance

✓ *Temporary life insurance*

✓ *Permanent life insurance*

- Whole life insurance
- Universal life insurance

How Life Insurance is Priced

✓ Mortality expectations

✓ Discount rate

✓ Loading

✓ *How much life insurance does one need?* ★

- The *primary purpose* of life insurance is to *replace the present value of future earnings*
- *Other reasons* to consider life insurance include the following：
  - *Immediate financial expenses*： funeral and legal expenses
  - *Legacy goals*
  - The insurance company's *ability to meet its financial obligations*

Comparisons of Life Insurance Costs ★ 计算 → 本质就是求先付年金 PMT

✓ Net payment cost index

- Cost *per year per 1000$*
- 投保期 20 年
- 假设投保人在 20 年后死亡

✓ Surrender cost index

- *Cost per year per 1000$*
- 投保期 20 年
- 假设投保人在 20 年后退保

Other Types of Insurance

Disability Income Insurance

✓ *Disability* 定义

- According to one's *regular occupation*
- According to any occupation is suited by *education* and *experience*
- According to duties of *any occupation*

✓ 术语

- *Benefit period*：Specifies *how long payments* will be made
- *Elimination period, or waiting period*：Specifies the *number of days the insured must be disabled before payments* begin being *made*
- *The rehabilitation clause*：Provides *payments* for *physical therapy* to help the disabled rejoin the workforce
- *The waiver of premium clause*：Specifies that premiums *need not be paid* if the insured becomes disabled

✓ 术语

- *A non-cancelable and guaranteed renewable policy*：Guarantees that the policy will be *renewed annually as long as premiums are paid* and that there will be *no changes to premiums* or promised disability benefits
- *A non-cancelable policy*：*Cannot be canceled as long as premiums are paid*，but the insurer can *increase premiums*
- *Inflation adjustments to benefits*：*Adjust benefits* with an accepted index

Other Types of Insurance（续）

Health/Medical Insurance

✓ *Common insurance types*

- *Indemnity plan*：Allows the insured to go to essentially *any medical service provider*
- *Preferred provider organization (PPO)*：Which is a large *network* of medical service *providers* that charge *lower prices* to individuals *within the plan*
- *Health maintenance organization (HMO)*：Allows office visits at no，or very little，cost to encourage individuals to seek help for *small medical problems*
- *Comprehensive major medical insurance*：Covers the *vast majority of health care expenses*

✓ 术语

- *Deductibles* refer to the amount of health care expenses that the *insured person must pay* in a year *before any* expense *reimbursement* is paid by the insurance company
- *Coinsurance* specifies the *percentage of any expense that the insurance company will pay*
- *Copayments* are *fixed payments that the insured must make for a particular service*，such as a doctor's office visit
- *Maximum out-of-pocket expense* refers to the *total amount of expenses* incurred within a year *beyond which the insurance company pays 100%*
- *Maximum yearly benefit* refers to the *maximum amount* that the insurance *company will pay in a year*
- *Maximum lifetime benefit*：The maximum amount that the insurance company will pay over an *individual's lifetime*
- *Preexisting conditions* refer to *health conditions* that the insured had when applying for insurance
- *Preadmission certification*：A requirement that the *insured receive approval* from the insurer *before treatment*

Annuities

Basic Concept

Four Parties to an Annuity Contract

- The *insurer*
- The *annuitant*
- The *contract owner*
- The *beneficiary*

Classification of Annuities

- Deferred variable annuities
- Deferred fixed annuities
- Immediate variable annuities
- Immediate fixed annuities
- Advanced Life Deferred Annuities (ALDA)

✓ *Increased demand for an annuity* ★

- *Longer-than-average* life expectancy
- Greater preference for *lifetime income*
- Less concern for *leaving money* to heirs
- More *conservative* investing preferences (i.e., greater risk aversion)
- Lower *guaranteed income* from other sources (such as pensions)
- The broad international shift away from defined benefit plans and toward *defined contribution plans* has increased the demand for annuities

第 4 章

Portfolio Management for Institutional Investors

Reading 13

MANAGING INSTITUTIONAL INVESTOR PORTFOLIOS

Pension Plans

Pension 种类

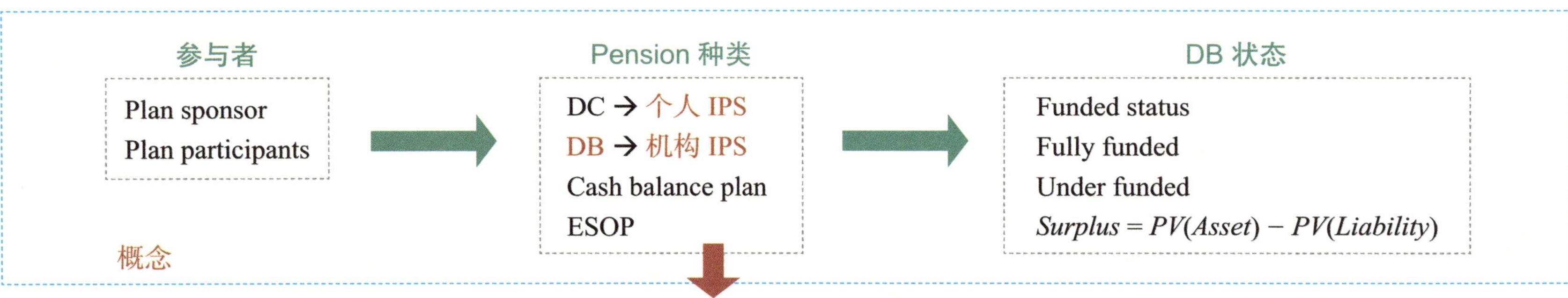

Plan types	Employer	Employee
DB 掌握区别★	• *Liability of employer* • Determined by stated criteria usually related to years of service and salary • Sponsor manage plan assets and *bear investment risk*	• Receive payments after retirement • Subject to "early termination" risk if employee is terminated early • *Not bear risk / return* of investment
DC	• Firm keeps all contributions current • Only financial liability is *making contributions* to employee's account • The plan must offer sufficient investment vehicles	• Own the plan and can transport account to other employment situations *(portable)* • *Bear all risk / return* of investment • Must make all investment decisions given available investment vehicles

Pension IPS

考的最多的机构 IPS

<table>
<tr><td rowspan="2">Return ★★</td><td>定性
● Required：Generate return sufficient to cover pension liabilities：$PV_A > PV_L$ ★
● Desired：Minimization of contributions ★
● Specific return requirement depends on funded status and contributions (assets) relative to accrued benefits (liabilities)</td></tr>
<tr><td>计算
● Fully funded：*Return requirement = Discount rate of plan liabilities*
● Under funded：*Return requirement = Discount rate of plan liabilities + excess return*</td></tr>
<tr><td rowspan="2">Risk ★★</td><td>影响 risk tolerance 的因素（increased risk tolerance）
● *Plan status*：Higher pension surplus
● *Sponsor financial status and profitability*：Low debt ratios and higher current and expected profitability
● Sponsor and pension fund common risk exposures：*The lower the correlation* of sponsor operating results with pension asset returns
● Plan features →*Early retirement & lump sum distribution* (lower risk tolerance)
● *Workforce characteristics* →The younger the workforce and the greater the proportion of active lives relative to retired lives</td></tr>
<tr><td>Risk objective
● *Minimize pension surplus volatility*
● *Minimize shortfall risk*</td></tr>
</table>

Liquidity ★	影响因素 ● Workforce mix → *Greater retired lives*， increased liquidity needs ● *Sponsor contributions* vs. benefit payments → Higher profitability reduces liquidity needs ● Plan features → *Early retirement or lump sum* provisions increase liquidity needs
	计算 ● *Liquidity requirement* = *Benefit payments − pension contributions*
Time Horizon ★	● Going concern (multistage) or is a terminated plan (single stage) ● Active lives → Time horizon associated with expected term to retirement ● Retired lives → A function of life expectancy for those currently receiving benefits
Legal and Regulatory	● Most countries federally regulate pension plans
Taxes	● Tax-exempt
Unique	● ERISA requires due diligence， but small sponsors may not have the plan resources or expertise to thoroughly investigate alternative assets

Foundations & Endowments

两者的区别

考试时两者的 IPS 基本相同

Foundations	Endowments
Typically grant-making institutions funded by gifts and investment assets (Ford，Rockefeller，and Gates foundations)	Long-term funds generally owned by operating non-profit institutions such as universities and colleges (Harvard，Yale and Princeton universities)

Endowment Spending Rate ★

Simple spending rule → $Spending_t = S\ (market\ value_{t-1})$

缺点：波动大

Rolling 3-year average spending rule → $Spending_t = (Spending\ rate)\left(\frac{market\ value_{t-1} + market\ value_{t-2} + market\ value_{t-3}}{3}\right)$

缺点：Extraordinary changes 影响

Geometric spending rule → $Spending_t = (R)\ (Spending_{t-1})\ (1+I_{t-1})+(1-R)\ (S)\ (market\ value_{t-1})$

优点：克服 extraordinary changes 的影响★

Foundations & Endowments IPS

<table>
<tr><td rowspan="2">Return ★★</td><td>定性：Provide perpetual support and the preservation of real purchasing power</td></tr>
<tr><td>计算：Return requirement = Required payout plus expected inflation and fund expenses</td></tr>
<tr><td rowspan="2">Risk ★★</td><td>Lower ability to tolerate risk if（影响因素）
● Higher spending rate
● Heavy reliance upon donations，10% or more its ability to tolerate risk is diminished
● Greater budget dependency
● No spending rule in place
● Smaller size of endowment</td></tr>
<tr><td>Risk objective
✓ More fluid，creative and aggressive than pension funds
✓ Above-average risk tolerance
● Because they have no contractually defined liability and long time horizon</td></tr>
</table>

Liquidity	• Anticipated and unanticipated needs for cash in excess of contributions received Low liquidity requirements（影响因素） • Spending needs vs. gifts and donations • Large cash outlays may sometimes be needed for capital improvements – new library • Care and discipline should be exercised in valuing illiquid，non-marketable investments estimates to determine spending
Time Horizon	• *Perpetuity*，usually very long
Legal and Regulatory	• Prudent Investor Rule generally applies
Taxes	• Non taxable，except UBIT — Unrelated business income
Unique	• Concentrated holdings. Socially responsible investing

Life Insurance Companies

Return ★	✓ Minimum return：Based on mortality rates ✓ Enhanced margin：Spread management (above credited rates) used to be more competitive ✓ Surplus → Focus on growth，taxable account
Risk ★	✓ Interest rate risk ● Valuation concerns：Surplus write-down → Lower risk tolerance (ability) ● Reinvestment risk：Reinvesting coupon income at a rate lower than the original ✓ Cash flow volatility ✓ Credit risk
Liquidity ★	✓ *Disintermediation → Int↑，liability durations ↓ & Asset-liability mismatch* ✓ Asset marketability risk
	Needing *minimal liquidity* because the *longer-term nature of liabilities*
Time Horizon	✓ Traditionally holding periods of 20 ～ 40 years ✓ Has become progressively shorter as the duration of liabilities has decreased
Legal and Regulatory	✓ Eligible investments ✓ Prudent Investor Rule ✓ Valuation Methods is mandated by the NAIC
Taxes	✓ Policyholder's share (not taxed) ✓ Corporate share，namely funds transferred to surplus (taxed)
Unique	✓ Concentration of product offerings，company size，and level of surplus

Non-life Insurance Companies

✓ Compare with life insurance company

- Non-life liability durations tend to be *shorter*，and claim processing and payments periods are *longer*，than for life companies
- In general，a life insurance company's liabilities are relatively certain in value but uncertain in timing，while a non-life insurance company's liabilities are relatively *uncertain in both value and timing*，with the result that non-life insurance companies are exposed to *more volatility* in their operating results

Return	✓ Greater uncertainty due to the possibility of higher claims frequency ✓ Not as interest rate sensitive since their policies do not typically pay periodic returns ✓ 分层 ● Maximize the return on their fixed-income portfolio for purposes of meeting (i.e., immunizing) claims ● Use returns from the equity portion of their portfolio to grow the surplus ● Use the surplus portfolio to provide funds for unexpected, large liability claims
Risk	✓ Limited risk tolerances ● Due to the relatively high uncertainty associated with claims ● The cash flow characteristics of nonlife companies are often erratic and unpredictable
Liquidity	✓ High liquidity requirements given the uncertainty of the cash flow
Time Horizon	✓ Shorter time horizons than life insurance companies
Legal and Regulatory	✓ Risk-Based Capital (RBC) requirements have been established
Taxes	✓ Taxable entities
Unique	✓ The current financial status of nonlife insurance companies, coupled with managing investment risk and liquidity requirements

Banks

Return	• Earn a positive interest spread
Risk	• ALM • Below average
Liquidity	• Deposit withdrawals • Demand for loans as well as regulation
Time Horizon	• Since most bank liabilities are short term，the average maturity of securities in the portfolio tends to be short to intermediate term (3 ～ 7 years)
Legal and Regulatory	• Are highly regulated
Taxes	• Taxable entities
Unique	• Vary from bank to bank

Bank risk measures

$$LADG = D_{Assets} - \left(\frac{L}{A}\right)D_{Liabilities}$$

✓ For an increase in interest rates

- If $LADG<0$， *market value of equity* increase ↑
- If $LADG>0$， *market value of equity* decrease ↓
- If $LADG=0$， *market value of equity* unchanged

✓ For an decrease in interest rates

- If $LADG<0$， *market value of equity* decrease ↓
- If $LADG>0$， *market value of equity* increase ↑
- If $LADG=0$， *market value of equity* unchanged

第 5 章

Applications of Economic Analysis to Portfolio Management

Reading 14

CAPITAL MARKET EXPECTATIONS

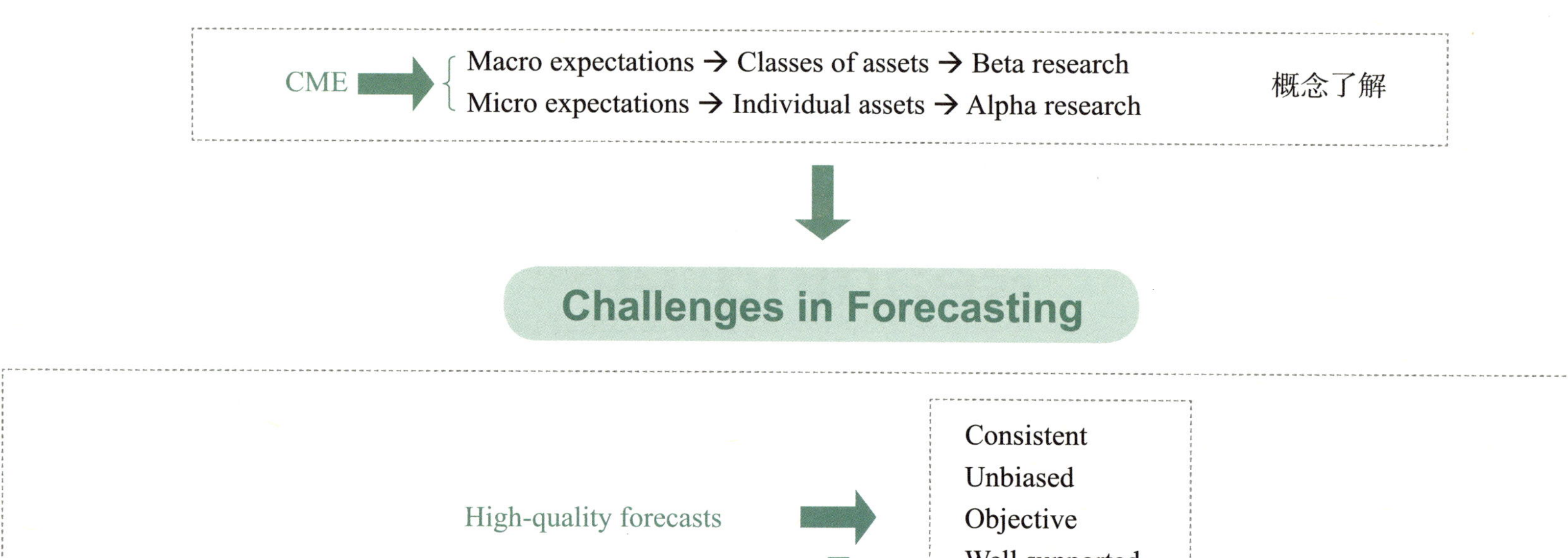
CME
Macro expectations → Classes of assets → Beta research
Micro expectations → Individual assets → Alpha research
概念了解
Challenges in Forecasting
High-quality forecasts
Consistent
Unbiased
Objective
Well supported
Minimum error
9 problems

Limitations to using economic data	• Time lag • Revision • Change in definition or calculation method • Re-based
Data measurement errors and biases	• Transcription errors • Survivorship bias ★ → *Return is overestimated* • Appraisal data ★ → *Without liquid public markets. risk is underestimated*
Limitation of historical estimates	• Nonstationarity ★ → *Cover multiple regimes*，用 *high-frequency data* 解决，但 ρ↓
Ex Post risk as a biased risk measure of Ex Ante risk ★	• Underestimate ex ante risk • Over estimate ex ante anticipated returns
Biases in analyst's methods	• Data-mining bias ★ → *Check for economic rationales. Use out-of-sample data* • Time-period bias ★
Ignore conditioning information	• Relationship between returns and economic variables change
Misinterpretation of correlations ★	• ρ 只代表相关关系，不代表因果；nonlinear relationship
6 Psychological traps	• The anchoring trap • The status quo trap • The confirming evidence trap • The overconfidence trap • The prudence trap • The recallability trap
Model and input uncertainty	• Model uncertainty & Input uncertainty

Micro Expectations

结构 →
- Formal Tools ★★ → 定量，计算
- Survey and Panel Methods → 问别人
- Judgment → 问自己

（Survey and Panel Methods、Judgment）定性 → 了解

预测 risk →

预测 return

Formal Tools	Details
Statistical tools	Projecting historical data → The arithmetic/geometric mean
	Shrinkage estimators → *Reduce (shrink) the influence of historical outliers*
	Time-Series Estimators (*Volatility clustering*)：$\sigma_t^2=\theta\sigma_{t-1}^2+(1-\theta)\varepsilon_t^2$，$0<\theta<1$
	Multifactor models ★ → 计算单个资产风险及两个资产的协方差 $\sigma_i^2=\beta_{i,1}^2\sigma_{F_1}^2+\beta_{i,2}^2\sigma_{F_2}^2+2\beta_{i,1}\beta_{i,2}\text{Cov}(F_1F_2)+\sigma_{\varepsilon,i}^2$ $\text{Cov}(i,j)=\beta_{i,1}\beta_{j,1}\sigma_{F_1}^2+\beta_{i,2}\beta_{j,2}\sigma_{F_2}^2+(\beta_{i,1}\beta_{j,2}+\beta_{i,2}\beta_{j,1})\text{Cov}(F_1F_2)$
DCF models	Grinold and Kroner model ★ → 计算，优点。可以分解为三部分： $\hat{R}_i=\dfrac{Div_1}{P_0}-\Delta S+i+g+\Delta\left(\dfrac{P}{E}\right)$ ● Expected income return：$D/P-\Delta S$ ● Expected nominal earnings growth return：$i+g$ ● Expected repricing return：$\Delta P/E$
Risk premium approach	● Equity risk premiums：$E(R)$ = *YTM on a long-term government bond + equity risk premium* ● Fixed income premiums：$E(R)$ = *Real risk free interest rate + inflation premium + default risk premium + illiquidity premium + maturity premium + tax premium*
Equilibrium models	ICAPM ★ → 计算，看书中例题即可 ● 调整：*+ liquidity premium；考虑 segmentation 的影响*

Macro Expectations

一国预测 → 经济周期预测★

✓ The measures of economic activity are

- *GDP*
- *The output gap*：The difference between potential GDP and actual GDP. A positive output gap is open，inflation tends to decline. Once the gap closes，inflation tends to rise
- *Recession*：A recession is a broad-based economic downturn

✓ Inventory cycle

- When the *inventory/sales ratio has moved down*，*the economy is likely to be strong* in the next few quarters

✓ The Yield Curve and Recessions

- The yield curve tends to flatten or become inverted prior to a recession

Five Phases of the Business Cycle

Phase	Economy	Fiscal and Monetary Policy	Confidence	Capital Markets
1.Initial recovery	Inflation still declining	Stimulatory fiscal policies	Confidence starts to rebound	Stock prices strongly rising
2.Early upswing	Healthy economic Growth inflation remains low		Increasing confidence	Short rates moving up Bond yields stable to up slightly Stock prices trending upward
3.Late upswing	Inflation gradually picks up	Policy becomes restrictive	Boom mentality	Short rates rising Bond yields rising Stocks topping out，often volatile
4.Slow-down	Inflation continues to accelerate Inventory correction begins		Confidence drops	Short-term interest rates peaking Bond yields topping out and starting to decline stocks declining
5.Recession	Production declines Inflation peaks		Confidence weak	Short rates declining Bond yields dropping Stocks bottoming and then starting to rise

Inflation/Deflation Effects on Asset Classes

	Cash	Bonds	Equity	Real Estate/ Other Real Assets
Inflation at or below expectations	Neutral	Neutral	Positive	Neutral
Inflation above expectations	Positive	Negative	Negative	Positive
Deflation	Negative	Positive	Negative	Negative

Monetary Policy：目标利率确定 → Taylor Rule

$$r_{target/optimal}=r_{neutral}+\left[0.5\times\left(GDPg_{forecast}-GDPg_{trend}\right)+0.5\times\left(i_{forecast}-i_{target}\right)\right]$$

Monetary Policy & Fiscal Policy 对 yield curve 的影响

		Fiscal Policy	
		Loose	Tight
Monetary Policy	Loose	Yield curve steep	Yield curve moderately steep
	Tight	Yield curve flat	Yield curve inverted

一国预测 → Economic Growth Trends

Trend growth in GDP → { Growth from labor inputs; Growth from labor productivity }

了解，在后面的 Reading 16 展开

4 Approaches to Forecasting Exchange Rates ★

判断升值贬值

Purchasing power parity	$\frac{E(S_t)}{S_0}=\left(\frac{1+\pi_X^e}{1+\pi_Y^e}\right)^t$，if t=1，$\frac{E(S_t)-S_0}{S_0}=\%\Delta S_{X/Y}\approx\pi_X^e-\pi_Y^e$ ✓ *The country with higher inflation will see its currency value decline*
Relative economic strength	✓ Favorable investment climate will attract investors，which will increase its value ✓ High short-term interest rates will attract investors who bid up the currency value over the short term
Capital flows	✓ 外资涌入 → 本币升值 ● Focus：*Equity investment or foreign direct investment (FDI)*
Savings-investment imbalances	✓ 研究本国储蓄与投资关系 ✓ $S<I$ → 引进外资 → 本币升值

Economic Forecasting 工具

掌握优缺点

Econometric analysis	Advantage	● Models can be quite robust with many factors used ● New data may be used within models to quickly generate output ● Provides quantitative estimates of economy changes
	Disadvantage	● Most complex and time-consuming to formulate ● Data inputs and relationships not easy to forecast and not static ● Requires careful analysis of output ● Rarely forecasts recessions well
Economic indicators	Advantage	● Usually intuitive and simple in construction ● May be available from third parties ● May be tailored for individual needs ● A literature exists on the effective use of various third-party indicators
	Disadvantage	● Relationships between inputs are not static ● Can provide false signals
A checklist approach	Advantage	● Limited complexity ● Flexible：Allows structural changes to be easily incorporated
	Disadvantage	● Subjective ● Time intensive to create ● Complexity has to be limited due to the manual nature of the process

Reading 15

EQUITY MARKET VALUATION

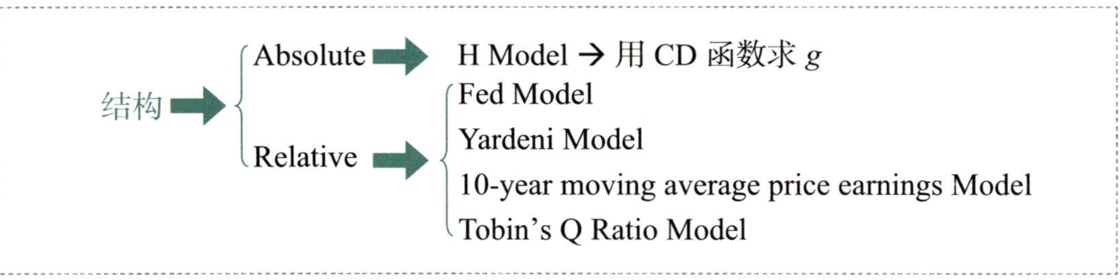
结构
Absolute
H Model → 用 CD 函数求 g
Relative
Fed Model
Yardeni Model
10-year moving average price earnings Model
Tobin's Q Ratio Model

Absolute → H Model

$$V_0 = \frac{D_0}{r - g_L}\left[(1+g_L) + \frac{N}{2}(g_S - g_L)\right]$$ 计算

求解 g 的方法

Cobb-Douglas Model ★

General expression $Y = AK^{\alpha}L^{\beta}$ ➡ $\frac{\Delta Y}{Y} \approx \frac{\Delta A}{A} + \alpha\frac{\Delta K}{K} + (1-\alpha)\frac{\Delta L}{L}$

Factor Increased ★★	Effect on Growth	Explanation
Savings rate	Increase	More capital available at reduced interest rates. Increased investment in capital stock
Labor force	Increase	Increase in labor force growth rate
Production efficiency	Increase	Increase in TFP
Environmental and pollution controls	Decrease	Retooling and other costs；possibly reduced and/or more expensive output
Children per household	Increase	Increase in labor force growth rate
Number of two-wageearner households	Increase	Increase in labor force growth rate
Retirement age	Increase	Increase in labor force growth rate
Import taxes/restrictions	Decrease	Increased costs；possibly reduced and/or more expensive output

Relative ★★

掌握判断方法及优缺点

Model	Details
Fed model	假设 $E_1/P_0 = R_{T\text{-}Bond}$，其中 $E_1 = E_0 \times (1+g)$ ● $E_1/P_0 > R_{T\text{-}Bond}$ → *undervalued* ● $E_1/P_0 < R_{T\text{-}Bond}$ → *overvalued*
	缺点 ● Ignore the *equity risk premium* ● Ignore earning *growth* opportunities ● Compares a *real* variable to a *nominal* variable
Yardeni model	$P_0 = \frac{E_1}{r-g} \Rightarrow \frac{E_1}{P_0} = r - g \qquad \frac{E_1}{P_0} = y_B - d \times LTEG$ If $\frac{E_1}{P_0} - [y_B - d \times (LTEG)] > 0 \Rightarrow$ market is under-valued
	缺点 ● The risk premium used is actually a measure of *default risk*，*not equity risk* ● The value investors place on earnings growth (d=0.1) is assumed to be constant ● The *growth rate* used in the model (LTEG) might not be an accurate estimate

Model	Details
10-year moving average price/ earnings	• Numerator：Real S&P 500 price index • Denominator：Moving average of the preceding 10 years of real reported earnings • *Both are adjusted for inflation using CPI* • 判断方法：Current value > historical average → *overpriced*
	优点 • It considers the effects of *inflation* • It captures the effects of *business cycles* 缺点 • It is *backward-looking* • It does not consider the effects of changes in *accounting rules* or methods • *Empirical studies* have found that very high or low P/10-year MA(E) ratios have persisted
Tobin's Q ratio	Tobin's Q ratio → market value of a company/ replacement cost of its assets 与 1 比较 • >1，资本市场贵 → stock overvalued • <1，资本市场便宜 → stock undervalued Equity Q → market value of equity/net asset value，与 1 比较
	缺点 • It is difficult to obtain an accurate measure of *replacement cost* for many assets • *Evidence suggests* that both low and high levels of Tobin's Q and Equity Q can persist

Top-down & Bottom-up Forecast ★

掌握结论

✓ Bottom-up forecasts are based on *consensus earnings estimates* from equity research analysts. Top-down estimates are often based on *econometric methods* rather than fundamental analysis

- If the belief exists that companies are reacting slowly to changes in economic conditions, then a market analyst may prefer a top-down forecast
- If the belief exists that the economy is on the *brink of a significant change*, then a market analyst may *prefer the bottom-up forecast*

✓ Bottom-up estimates may be *more optimistic* than top-down *heading into a recession*, and *more pessimistic* than top-down *coming out*

第 6 章

Asset Allocation and Related Decisions in Portfolio Management

Reading 16

INTRODUCTION TO ASSET ALLOCATION

The Investment Governance Background to Asset Allocation

了解

Investment governance is *the structure* that is expected to ensure that assets are invested to achieve the *asset owner's investment objectives within the asset owner's risk tolerance and constraints* and in compliance with *all applicable laws and regulations*

Elements of effective investment governance

- *Articulate the long and short-term objectives* of the investment program
- *Allocate decision rights and responsibilities* among the functional units in the governance hierarchy effectively
- Specify processes for developing and approving the *investment policy statement*
- Specify processes for developing and approving the program's *strategic asset allocation*
- Establish a *reporting framework* to monitor the program's progress toward the agreed-on goals and objectives
- Periodically undertake a *governance audit*

The Economic Balance Sheet and Asset Allocation ★★

计算

Conventional assets and liabilities	Financial assets and financial liabilities E.g., equity, fixed-income security, alternative investment
Extended portfolio assets and liabilities	**Extended portfolio assets** • *Human capital* (The PV of future earnings), *the PV of pension income, and the PV of expected inheritances* **Extended portfolio liabilities** • PV of future consumption, education cost, PV of expected future support to university

Strategic Asset Allocation

Main characteristics

- *Combines capital market expectations and the investment objectives*， and investment *constraints*
- *Long-term* in nature， *targets* portfolio and *policy portfolio*

Three Broad Approaches in Asset Allocation ★

结论

Asset-only approach	
Basic principle	✓ *Focus solely* on the *asset side* ✓ Selecting portfolios that *make efficient use of asset risk* ✓ *Mean-variance optimization* ✓ Sharpe ratio is *a key descriptor* of an asset allocation. The limitations of Sharpe ratio ● It does *not capture other characteristics* ● It *cannot confirm that the absolute level of portfolio risk* is within the range ● Higher Sharpe ratio of an asset may *not improve the portfolio's Sharpe ratio*
Global market portfolio in asset-only approaches	*As a baseline of* asset allocation ✓ It is the *portfolio that minimizes non-diversifiable risk* ✓ It mitigate any investment biases， such as *home-country bias*

Liability-relative approach 结论

- Dedicating assets to *meet*, *respectively*, *legal liabilities and quasi-liabilities*
- A typical use of *fixed-income assets* in liability-relative asset allocation

Compare AO with liability-relative approaches to DB plan ★★	
Asset-only approaches	● Involve a higher allocation to global equities ● *A decline in equity values* would put the plan into *underfunded status* ● *Creates contribution risk* for the plan sponsor
Liability-relative approaches	● An allocation to a *fixed-income* portfolio that is very *closely matched with liability* risk exposures ● The equities allocation can provide potential for increasing the size of the buffer between pension assets and liabilities *with negligible risk to funded status*

Goals-based approach ★★★

Identify Goals

- Range from supporting lifestyle needs to aspirational needs. E.g., *Personal risk bucket*, *market risk bucket*, *and aspirational risk bucket*

Construct Sub-Portfolios

问题：这个 allocation 可以满足哪一个 goal？重要问题!

- If the portfolio invest more cash and bond, *it stresses liquidity and stability*, which may be appropriate to *meet short-term lifestyle and education goals*
- If the portfolio invest more equity, *it has a greater growth emphasis*, which may be appropriate to *funding the long-term and desired goals*

The Overall Portfolio

Distinctions Between Liabilities and Goals ★

Liabilities	Goals
Liabilities of institutional investors are *legal obligation or debts*	Goals, such as meeting lifestyles or aspirational objectives are *not legal*
Institutional liabilities are *uniform in nature*	Individual's goals may *be many and varied*
Liabilities of institutional investor may often *be forecast with confidence*	Individual goals are not subject to the law of large numbers

Relevant Objectives and Risk Concepts ★★

Asset Allocation Approach	Relation to Economic Balance Sheet	Typical Objective	Typical Uses and Asset Owner Types	Relevant Risk Concepts
Asset-only	Does not explicitly model liabilities or goals	*Maximize Sharpe ratio* for acceptable level of volatility	Liabilities or goals are not defined and/or simplicity is important • Some *foundations*, *endowments* • *Sovereign wealth funds* • Individual investors	• *Volatility of the portfolios return (standard deviation)* as a primary measure of risk • Incorporate other risk sensitivities, such as *tracking risk and Downside risk*
Liability-relative	Models legal and quasi-liabilities	*Fund liabilities* and invest excess assets for growth	Penalty for not meeting liabilities high • *Banks* • *Defined benefit pensions* • *Insurers*	• *Shortfall risk*
Goals-based	Models goals	*Achieve goals* with *specified required probabilities of success*	• *Individual* investors	• The risk of falling to achieve goals. E.g., *the maximum acceptable probability of not achieving a goal*

Modeling Asset Class Risk

Criteria for Asset Class Specification ★★★ 重要性质

Principles	Example
Assets *within an asset class* should be relatively *homogeneous*, and have similar attributes	Defining *equities to include both real estate and common stock* would result in a non-homogeneous asset class
Asset classes should be *mutually exclusive. Overlapping asset classes will reduce the effectiveness* in controlling risk	*Domestic equities and ex-US* are more appropriate, but *domestic equities and* global equities are not
Asset classes should be diversifying. An included asset class *should not have extremely high expected correlations with other asset classes*	In general, a pariwise correlation above 0.95 is undesirable
The asset classes as a group should cover the majority of world investable wealth	Complete
Absorb a meaningful proportion of an investor's portfolio	*Liquidity and transaction costs* should be considered

Factor-Based Approach ★

Asset Class-based Asset Allocation and Factor-based Asset Allocation	
Asset class-based asset allocation	Use *asset classes* as the basis for portfolio construction ● Tends to *obscure the portfolio's sensitivity to overlapping risk factors*, so controlling risk exposures may be problematic
Factor-based asset allocation	Bear on the issue of controlling systematic risk exposures in asset allocation

The use of risk factors in asset allocation: *Factors are not directly investable*. Both *long and short positions isolate the respective risks and associated expected return premiums (zero (dollar) investment, or self-financing investment)*

- *Inflation.* Going long nominal Treasuries and short inflation-linked bonds isolates the inflation component
- *Real interest rates.* Inflation-linked bonds provide a proxy for real interest rates
- *US volatility.* VIX (Chicago Board Options Exchange Volatility Index) futures provide a proxy for implied volatility
- *Credit spread.* Going long high-quality credit and short Treasuries/government bonds isolates credit exposure
- *Duration.* Going long 10+year Treasuries and short 1 ～ 3 year Treasuries isolates the duration exposure being targeted
- *Mortgage.* Mortgage-backed — Treasury bonds
- *Market.* Total market return — Cash
- *Size.* Small cap — Large cap
- *Valuation.* Value — Growth

Implementation Choices and Rebalancing

Implementation Choices

1. Passive/Active Choices at Asset Level → *Tactical asset allocation* ★

Features of TAA

- *Deliberate short-term deviations* from SAA *within rebalancing ranges or within risk budgets*
- Involve *market timing* as it involves buying and selling in anticipation of short-term changes in market direction

Disadvantages of TAA

- TAA is a *source of risk*
- Key barriers to successful tactical asset allocation are *monitoring and trading costs*

2. Passive/Active within Asset Classes → *Passive/Active spectrum* ★

Factors Influence Decisions on Passive/Active Investment

- Available investments
- Scalability of active strategies being considered
- The feasibility of investing passively while incorporating client-specific constraints
- Beliefs concerning market informational efficiency
- The trade-off of *expected incremental benefits* relative to *incremental costs and risks* of active choices
- Tax status. *Active investments* would be held in available *tax-advantaged accounts*

Examples

- *GDP-weighted global bond index*. The *passive choice is represented by the overall selection of the universe of global bonds*. However, the *active choice is represented by the weighting scheme*
- *Volatility-weighted global bond index*. The active element is the decision to *overweight securities with low volatility and underweight securities with high volatility*

Rebalancing

Calendar rebalancing: Rebalancing *on a periodic basis*; lower overhead

Percent-range rebalancing: *Setting rebalancing points*; *a more disciplined risk policy*

Factors Affecting the Optimal Corridor Width of an Asset Class ★★★

Factors	Effect on Corridor Width	Explanation
Factors positively related to optimal corridor width		
Transaction costs	The higher the transaction costs, the wider the optimal corridor	High transaction costs set a high hurdle rate for rebalancing benefits to overcome
Tax rates on CG	The higher tax rates should also be associated with wider corridors	For taxable investors, transactions trigger capital gains in jurisdictions that tax them
Risk tolerance	The higher the risk tolerance, the wider the optimal corridor	High risk tolerance means less sensitivity to divergences from the target allocation
Correlation with rest of portfolio	The higher the correlation, the wider the optimal corridor	When asset classed move in sync, further divergence from target weights is less likely
Factors negatively related to optimal corridor width		
Asset class volatility	The higher the asset class volatility, the narrower the optimal corridor	High volatility relative to the rest means more likelihood to diverge from original allocation
Volatility of rest of portfolio	The higher the volatility of rest of portfolio, the narrower the optimal corridor	High volatility of the rest means more likelihood to diverge from original allocation
Liquidity	*Illiquid*: *wider* rebalancing ranges. Rebalancing of an illiquid asset may be *rebalanced indirectly*	
Beliefs in momentum favor *wider* rebalancing ranges, whereas *mean reversion* encourages *tighter* ranges		

Reading 17

PRINCIPLES OF ASSET ALLOCATION

Asset-only Asset Allocations

1. Mean-variance Optimization ★★★

基本方法 →

Maximize the expected return of the portfolio for an expected level of risk

- Inputs：*Returns*，*risks(standard deviations)*，and pair-wise *correlations*

The objective function：Maximize $U_P = E(R_P) - 0.005\,\lambda\sigma_P^2$ 计算

- *The risk aversion coefficient(λ)* characterizes the investor's *risk-return trade-off*

Maximize SFR：$[E(R_P)-R_L]/\sigma_P$

实务中的问题 →

Constraint	• Budget constraint (or unity constraint)：The weights to sum to 1 • Allows only positive weights → *Corner Portfolios*
Time Horizon	• *"Single-period" framework*
Cash and Cash Equivalents	• *Separates out cash equivalents as a risk-free asset* → Combinations of the *risk-free asset with the tangency portfolio (highest Sharpe ratio)* • *Include cash in the optimization*
Economic B/S	Taking such extended assets and liabilities into *asset allocation decisions*

Criticisms →

- The outputs (asset allocations) are *highly sensitive to small changes in the inputs*
- The asset allocations tend to be *highly concentrated* in a subset of the available asset classes
- Many investors are *concerned about more than the mean and variance of* returns
- The *sources of risk may not be diversified*
- MVO allocations are not directly connected to the value of the *liability*
- MVO is a *single-period framework*

2. Monte Carlo Simulation ★★★ → 解决 *single-period framework*

Strengths

- Monte Carlo Simulation *complements MVO* by *addressing the limitations of MVO as a single-period framework* and formulating the *multi-period problem*
- Monte Carlo Simulation can help *paint a realistic picture of potential future outcomes* when investor's *risk tolerance is either unknown*
- Investigate the effects of *trading/rebalancing costs* and *taxes*
- Monte Carlo Simulation can solve *path dependent* problem

解释 MCS 的结果

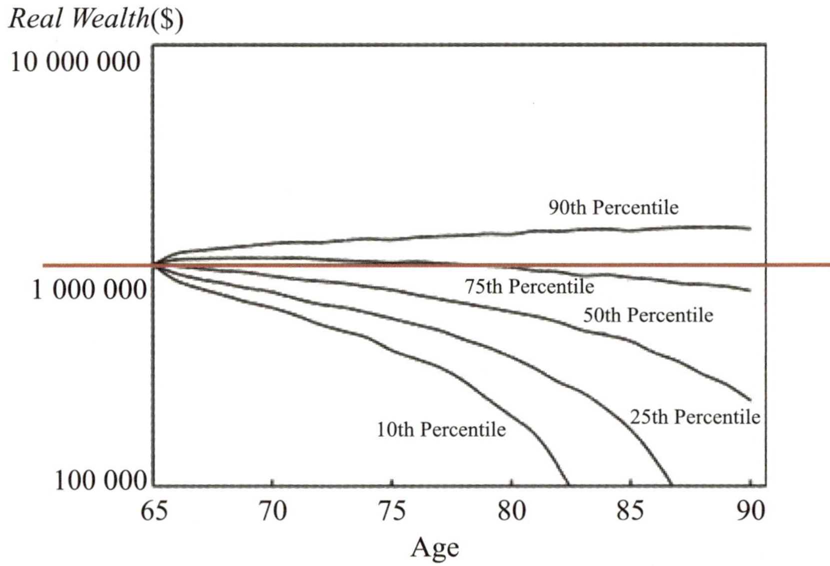

The median terminal (at age 90) value of the retirement portfolio is less than CAF$1 million

3. Reverse Optimization & 4. Black-Litterman Method ★★★ → 解决 ***highly sensitive to the inputs***

Strengths of Reverse Optimization →

- Take as its inputs *a set of asset allocation weights that are assumed to be optimal* and *solves for expected returns*, which are referred to as *implied or imputed returns*
- Relate assets' expected returns to their *systematic risk*

Criticisms of Reverse Optimization →

- Portfolio manager often have *alternative forecasts or views* regarding the expected return of the asset classes that differ from the returns implied by reverse optimization

↓

Black-Litterman Method → ***reflect an investor's own distinctive views***

Strengths of Black-Litterman Method

- It enables investors to *combine their unique forecasts of expected returns with reverse-optimized returns*
- Lead to *well-diversified asset allocations*

5. Adding Constraints Beyond the Budget Constraints → 解决 ***highly concentrated of MVO portfolio***

There are two primary reasons

(1) To incorporate *real-world constraints* into the optimization problem

(2) To help *overcome some of the potential shortcomings of mean-variance optimization*

6. Resampled Mean–Variance Optimization ★★ → 解决 ***highly sensitive to the inputs***

Strengths →

- Resampling *uses Monte Carlo Simulation* to estimate a large number of potential capital market assumptions and *averaged simulated frontiers*
- *More-diversified asset allocations*

Criticisms →

(1) Some frontiers have *concave "bumps"*

(2) The "riskier" asset allocations are *over-diversified*

(3) The asset allocations inherit the *estimation errors* in the original inputs

(4) The approach *lacks a foundation in theory*

7. Other Non-Normal Optimization Approaches ★ → 解决 ***MVO 只关心 mean and variance***

- MVO assume that many investors are only *concerned about the mean and variance.* Investor preferences may concern the third and fourth moments—*skewness and kurtosis*
- The *asymmetrical risk preferences* observed in investors

8. Allocating to Less Liquid Asset Classes

Unique challenges

(1) Due to the lack of accurate indexes, it is more challenging to make capital market assumptions for these less liquid asset classes

(2) Even if there were accurate indexes, there are *no low-cost passive investment vehicles* to track them

9. Risk Budgeting & 10. Factor-Based Asset Allocation ★★ → 解决 *sources of risk may not be diversified*

Aspects to risk budgeting

- The risk budget *identifies the total amount of risk* and *allocates the risk*
- An optimal risk budget *allocates* risk *efficiently*. The *process of finding the optimal risk budget* is risk budgeting

Risk Parity Asset Allocation	Optimal Use of Risk in The Pursuit of Return
Each asset should contribute equally to the total risk of the portfolio • $w_i \times Cov(r_i, r_p) = 1/n \times \sigma_p^2$ • Investors with a *greater appetite for risk* than the market as a whole would *borrow money to lever up*	*The ratio of excess return (over the risk-free rate) to MCTR is the same for all assets* • $MCTR_i$ = *Beta of asset class i with respect to portfolio* × *Portfolio return volatility* • $ACTR_i = Weight_i \times MCTR_i$

Liability-relative Asset Allocation ★★★

Characteristics of Liabilities that can Affect Asset Allocation

1. Fixed versus contingent cash flows
2. Legal versus quasi-liabilities
3. Duration and convexity of liability cash flows
4. Value of liabilities as compared with the size of the sponsoring organization
5. Factors driving future liability cash flows (inflation， economic conditions， interest rates， risk premium)
6. Timing considerations， such as longevity risk
7. Regulations affecting liability cash flow calculations

Characteristics of the Three Liability-Relative Asset Allocation Approaches

Surplus Optimization	Hedging/Return-Seeking Portfolios	Integrated Asset-Liability Portfolios
Simplicity	Simplicity	Increased *complexity*
Linear correlation	Linear or non-linear correlation	Linear or non-linear correlation
All levels of risk	*Conservative* level of risk	All levels of risk
Any funded ratio	*Positive funded ratio* for *basic* approach	Any funded ratio
Single period	Single period	*Multiple periods*

Comparing the Three Approaches to Liability-relative Asset Allocation	
Surplus optimization	• A straightforward *extension of the traditional (asset-only) mean-variance* model • The *assumptions* are *similar* to those of the *traditional Markowitz model*, where the *inputs are expected returns and a covariance* matrix • *Link* assets and the present value of liabilities through a *correlation* coefficient • *Surplus optimization* considers the asset allocation problem in *one step* • *Surplus optimization* does *not require an overfunded status*
Hedging/return-seeking portfolios approach (two-portfolio model)	• Does not require this input of *expected returns and a covariance* matrix • Divides asset allocation into *two steps* • The *basic approach* is *most appropriate for conservative investors*, such as overfunded/fully funded DB. *Underfunded investors* must apply *variants* of the two-portfolio approach (*Partial hedge & Dynamic versions*) • *Simplicity*
Integrated asset-liability approach	• The *most comprehensive* of the three • It requires a *formal method. Asset and liability decisions can be integrated and jointly optimized* • This approach can be implemented in a *factor-based model* • It has the *potential to improve* the institution's overall *surplus* • It does *not require* the *linear correlation* assumption and is *capable* of *modeling* transaction *costs*, turnover constraints, and other real-world *constraints* • The *capital required* for this approach is often determined by reference to the output of integrated asset-liability systems in banks

Goals-Based Asset Allocations ★★★

	Institutions (Liability)	Individuals
Goals	Single	*Multiple*
Time horizon	Single	Multiple
Risk measure	Volatility (return or surplus)	Probability of missing goal
Return determination	Mathematical expectations	*Minimum expectations*
Risk determination	Top-down/Bottom-up	*Bottom-up*
Tax status	Single，often tax-exempt	Mostly taxable

Step 1：Describing Client Goals

One seeks to achieve：*Needs*，*wants*，*wishes*，*and dreams*. Examples：

- They *need* a 95% chance of being able to maintain their current expenditures over the next five years
- They *want* an 85% chance of being able to maintain their current expenditures over the ensuing 25 years
- They *wish* to have a 75% chance to be able to create a family foundation one seeks to avoid：*Nightmares*，*fears*，*worries*，*and concerns*

Step 2: Constructing Sub-Portfolios (Selecting a Module) 重要问题!

"Highest Probability-and Horizon-Adjusted Return" Sub-Portfolio Module

Annualized Minimum Expectation Returns						
Time Horizon (years)	5					
Required Success						
99%	1.5%	0.9%	0.2%	−0.6%	−2.4%	−4.3%
95%	2.3%	2.2%	2.0%	1.7%	0.7%	−0.5%
90%	2.7%	3.0%	3.0%	2.9%	2.3%	1.5%
75%	3.5%	4.2%	4.6%	4.9%	5.0%	4.9%
Time Horizon (years)	10					
Required Success						
99%	2.3%	2.2%	2.0%	1.7%	0.7%	−0.5%
90%	3.2%	3.7%	4.0%	4.1%	4.0%	3.6%
75%	3.7%	4.6%	5.1%	5.6%	5.9%	6.0%
60%	4.1%	5.2%	5.9%	6.6%	7.2%	7.7%

Annualized Minimum Expectation Returns						
Time Horizon (years)	20					
Required Success						
95%	3.3%	3.9%	4.2%	4.4%	4.4%	4.1%
90%	3.5%	4.3%	4.7%	5.0%	5.2%	5.1%
85%	3.7%	4.5%	5.0%	5.4%	5.7%	5.8%
75%	3.9%	4.9%	5.5%	6.0%	6.5%	6.8%
Time Horizon (years)	25					
Required Success						
95%	3.4%	4.1%	4.4%	4.7%	4.7%	4.6%
90%	3.6%	4.4%	4.9%	5.2%	5.5%	5.5%
85%	3.7%	4.6%	5.2%	5.6%	6.0%	6.1%
75%	3.9%	4.9%	5.6%	6.2%	6.7%	7.0%

- For example, at a 10-year horizon and a 90% required probability of success, *Module D* would be selected to address a goal with this time horizon and required probability of success because its 4.1% expected return is higher than those of all the other modules. Thus, Module D offers the *lowest "funding cost" for the given goal*
- The US$6 671 000 required capital reflects the discounting of a US$10 million payment in 10 years at the 4.1%

Step 3：The Overall Portfolio

	Total Financial Assets					25 000
	Goals					
	1	2	3	4	Surplus	Overall Asset Allocation
Horizon (years)	5	25	10	20		
Required probability of success	95%	85%	90%	75%	$E(R_t)$	7.1%
Discount rate	2.3%	6.1%	4.1%	6.8%	$\sigma(R_t)$	7.6%

Module	A	F	D	F	C	
Required capital						
In currency	2 430	4 978	6 671	2 426	8 495	25 000
As a % of total	9.7%	19.9%	26.7%	9.7%	34.0%	100.0%

Step 4：Periodically Revisiting the Overall Asset Allocation

Heuristics and Other Approaches to Asset Allocation ★

The "120 minus your age" rule	• *120 – Age = Percentage allocated to stocks* • No theoretic basis for this heuristic；it results in a linear decrease in equity exposure that fit the general equity glide paths
The 60/40 stock/bond heuristic	• *60% equities and 40% fixed income* • The global financial asset market portfolio is close to 60/40 split
The 1/*N* rule：Equally weighting allocations to assets	• *Sidesteps problems of estimation error in inputs*
The endowment model (Yale Model) ★★	• Emphasize *large allocations to non-traditional investments* • The approach characteristically seeks to *earn illiquidity premiums* • In contrast to the endowment model is the asset allocation approach of *Norway's Government Pension Fund Global—passive investment* in publicly traded securities
Risk parity asset allocation	Each asset should contribute equally to the total risk of the portfolio：$w_i \times \text{Cov}(r_i, r_p) = 1/n \times \sigma_p^2$

Reading 18

ASSET ALLOCATION WITH REAL-WORLD CONSTRAINTS

Constraints in Asset Allocation ★

看原版书（讲义）例题

<table>
<tr><td rowspan="2">Asset size</td><td>Larger asset size</td><td>Economies of scale
● Have sufficient governance to invest the more complex asset classes
● Have sufficient size to build a diversified portfolio
Diseconomies of scale
● Exhaust the capacity of active external investment managers in certain asset classes and strategies
● Greater price impact</td></tr>
<tr><td>Small asset size</td><td>● Typically institutions with less than US$500 million in assets， and private wealth investors with less than US$25 million in assets
● To illiquid asset and alternative investment， smaller asset owners may need to implement via a commingled vehicle because their limited investment understanding/expertise and limited staff resources</td></tr>
<tr><td>Liquidity needs</td><td colspan="2">● The liquidity needs of the asset owner
● The liquidity characteristics of the asset classes in the opportunity set</td></tr>
<tr><td>Time horizon</td><td colspan="2">● As time progresses， the character of both assets (human capital) and liabilities changes
● Time horizon is also likely to affect the manner in which an investor prioritizes certain goals and liabilities</td></tr>
<tr><td>Regulatory and other external considerations</td><td colspan="2">● Local laws and regulations can have a material effect
● There may be cultural or religious factors which also constrain the asset allocation choices</td></tr>
</table>

Asset Allocation for the Taxable Investor ★★

看原版书（讲义）例题

After-Tax Portfolio Optimization

- Expected after-tax return：$r_{at}=p_d r_{pt}(1-t_d)+p_a r_{pt}(1-t_{cg})$
- Expected after-tax standard deviation：$\sigma_{at}=\sigma_{pt}(1-t)$
- Correlation：Do not need to be adjusted

If an asset class with *heavier tax burden*，it will *significantly reduce* in the allocation

Taxes and Portfolio Rebalancing

Rebalancing ranges for a *taxable portfolio* can be *wider*：$R_{at}=R_{pt}/(1-t)$

Strategies to Reduce Tax Impact

Tax-loss harvesting	Intentionally trading to *realize a capital loss*
Strategic asset location	✓ *Placing (or locating) less tax-efficient assets in accounts with more favorable tax treatment*, such as retirement savings accounts ● *Allocation to high-yield bonds and dividend-paying stocks* in her *tax-exempt* retirement portfolio ✓ One important *exception* to this general rule regarding asset location applies to assets held for *near-term liquidity needs*

Revising the Strategic Asset Allocation 了解

Trigger a special review of the asset allocation policy	
Change in goals	• Changes in business conditions • A change in the investor's personal circumstances
Change in constraints	• Changes in the expected payments from the fund • A significant cash inflow or unanticipated expenditure • Changes in regulations，time horizon and asset size
Change in beliefs	• Changes in the economic environment and capital market expectations • A change in trustees or committee members

Short-term Shifts in Asset Allocation (TAA) 了解

Evaluation

Performance of TAA *relative to SAA*

- Sharpe ratio
- Information ratio or the *t*-statistic
- Plotting the realized return and risk

Disadvantages

- *Additional costs*—higher trading costs and taxes
- Increase the *concentration of risk*

Two broad approaches

- *Discretionary TAA*：*qualitative* interpretation
- *Systematic TAA*：*quantitative* signals

Behavioral Biases in Asset Allocation 了解

Behavioral Biases	Description	Consequence	Overcoming
Loss aversion	Utility derived from a gain is much lower than the utility given up with an equivalent loss	• Assigns a greater weight to the negative outcomes • *Herding behavior* (institution)	*Framing risk* in terms of shortfall probability
The illusion of control	Overestimate one's ability to control events	*More frequent trading (TAA), greater concentration. Excessive use of leverage*	• Use *global market portfolio* as starting point • A *formal* asset allocation process
Mental accounting	Treat one sum of money differently from another	• *Goals-based investing* • *Concentrated stock positions*	Assigning the concentrated stock position to an aspirational goal
Recency bias ★	Overweight the importance of the *most recent observations*	*Tactical shifts* in asset allocation	*An objective* asset allocation *process* with pre-specified allowable ranges and *a strong governance framework*

Behavioral Biases	Description	Consequence	Overcoming
Framing	Answer a question differently based solely on the way in which it is asked	• Choice of an asset allocation may be influenced merely by the manner *in which the risk-to-return trade-off is presented* • Common in committee-oriented decision-making processes	Presenting the possible asset allocation choices with *multiple perspectives on the risk/reward trade-off*
Availability bias	Estimation based on how easily the outcome comes to mind	• *Familiarity bias* → *home bias* • Fall into the trap of *comparing their investment decisions (and performance) to others'*	• Using the *global market portfolio* as the starting point • *Avoiding comparison* of investment returns or asset allocation decisions with others

Reading 19

CURRENCY MANAGEMENT： AN INTRODUCTION

Foreign Exchange Concepts

Concept	Details
Base currency	Long & Short 都针对分母上的币种
Bid/Asked rule	Spot USD/EUR：1.3648/1.3652，30 days forward premium/discount =−5.6/−5.1 → 能读懂含义 重点：AUD/EUR，sell EUR=buy AUD

Using Derivatives in Currency Risk Management ★

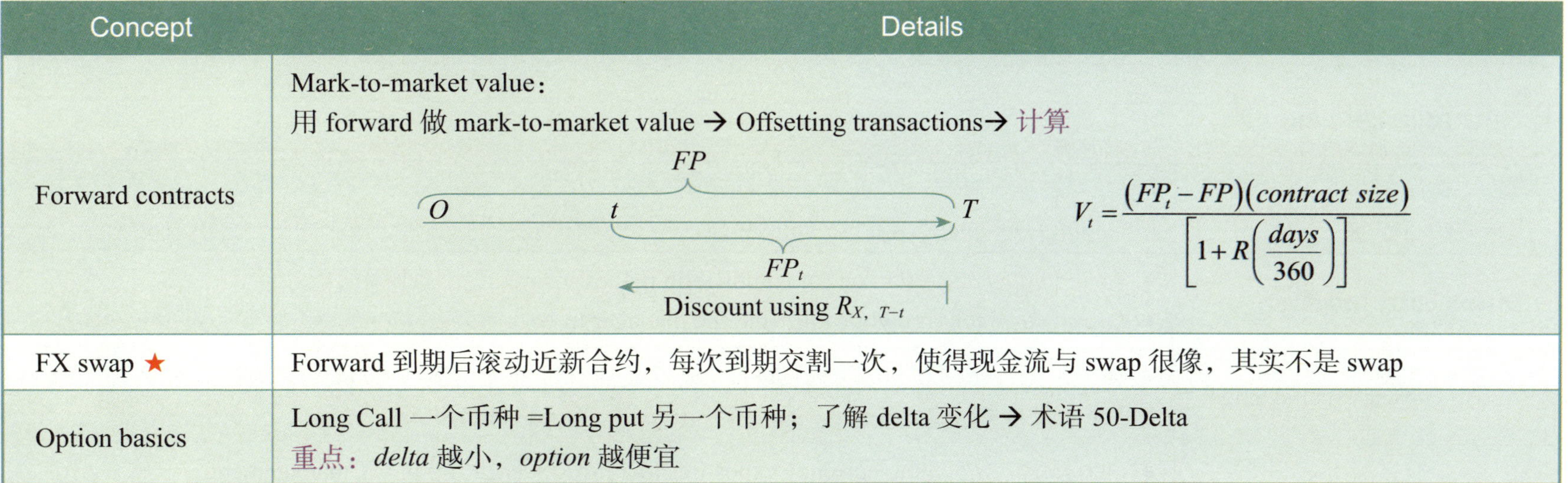

Concept	Details
Forward contracts	Mark-to-market value： 用 forward 做 mark-to-market value → Offsetting transactions→ 计算 FP; O, t, T; FP_t; Discount using $R_{X,\ T-t}$ $V_t = \frac{(FP_t - FP)(contract\ size)}{\left[1+R\left(\frac{days}{360}\right)\right]}$
FX swap ★	Forward 到期后滚动近新合约，每次到期交割一次，使得现金流与 swap 很像，其实不是 swap
Option basics	Long Call 一个币种 =Long put 另一个币种；了解 delta 变化 → 术语 50-Delta 重点：*delta* 越小，*option* 越便宜

外汇投资 Return & Risk ★★

Return 计算

- 单一资产 → $R_{DC}=(1+R_{FC})(1+R_{FX})-1=R_{FC}+R_{FX}+(R_{FC})(R_{FX})$
- 资产组合 → $R_{DC}=\sum_{i=1}^{n}w_i(R_{DC,i})$

Risk 计算

- $\sigma^2(R_{DC})\approx\sigma^2(R_{FC})+\sigma^2(R_{FX})+2\sigma(R_{FC})\sigma(R_{FX})\rho(R_{FC},R_{FX})$
- 投资国外 r_f→ $\sigma(R_{DC})=\sigma(R_{FX})\times(1+R_{FC})$

特例：hedged return and risk

$$R_{FX}=\frac{F-S_0}{S_0}$$

$$\sigma(R_{DC})=\sigma(R_{FC})\times(1+R_{FX})$$

Currency Management ★★

1. Strategic Decisions

Currency management strategies → 还要取决于客户 IPS	
Passive hedging	Matching benchmark currency exposures，*minimize tracking errors relative to the benchmark*
Discretionary hedging	• *Some limited discretion* on actual portfolio risk exposures（比较小幅偏离） • *Lessen currency risk* while allowing the manager to *earn modest incremental currency rewards*
Active currency management	• *Express directional opinions*，but is *nonetheless kept within mandated risk limits* • The goal is to *create incremental return (alpha)*，not to reduce risk
Currency overlay（外包）	• *Outsourced managing* currency exposures to a firm *specializing* in FX management • Treat currency as an *independent asset class* and take *directional* views on future currency movements

Cost considerations ★	
Trading costs	• The *bid/asked transaction cost* • *Purchasing options to hedge* • *Forward currency contracts*: *Rolling* hedges will typically generate *cash inflows or outflows* • *Overhead costs* is high
Opportunity costs	To be 100% hedging is to forgo any possibility of favorable currency rate moves-*opportunity cost*

Factors shift the strategic decision formulation ★
The strategic currency positioning should be biased toward a *more fully hedged* currency management program the *more*: 1. A *short term investment* objectives 2. *Risk averse* the beneficial owners of the portfolio are (and *unconcerned* with ex post regret over *missed opportunities*) 3. Immediate the income and/or *liquidity needs* of the portfolio 4. *Bond* exposure are held in a foreign-currency portfolio 5. *Cheaply* a hedging program can be implemented 6. *Volatile* (i.e., risky) financial markets are 7. *Skeptical* the beneficial owners and/or management oversight committee are of the expected benefits of active currency management

2. Tactical Currency Management→ 利用汇率风险获得 α

Economic fundamentals	Assumes that，in the long term，currency value will converge to fair value
Technical analysis	✓ Historical price data can be helpful in projecting future price movements ✓ Historical patterns in the price data have a tendency to repeat ✓ Does not attempt to determine where market prices should trade
A carry trade	✓ Borrowing in a lower interest rate currency and investing the proceeds in a higher *r* ✓ The carry trade is based on a *violation of uncovered interest rate parity (UCIRP)* and trading the *forward rate bias* ✓ *Carry trade and forward rate bias* ● *Implementing the carry trade*：Borrow low-yield，invest high-yield currency ● *Trading the forward rate bias*：Borrow forward premium currency，invest High-yield currency ✓ Risk of carry trade ● These High-yield currency advantages can be erased quickly，particularly if global financial markets are subject to *sudden bouts of stress* ● The carry trade is a *leveraged position*
Volatility trading	✓ Long straddle：*Long* at-the-money *call and put*，manager expecting *volatility to increase* ✓ Short straddle：*Short* an at-the-money call and put，volatility to *decrease* ✓ Strangle：*Out-of-the-money calls and puts*

	Expectations	Action
Relative Currency	Appreciation	Reduce the hedge on or increase the long position in the currency
	Depreciation	Increase the hedge on or decrease the long position in the currency
Volatility	Rising	Long straddle (or strangle)
	Falling	Short straddle (or strangle)
Market Conditions	Stable	A carry trade
	Crisis	Discontinue the carry trade

Tools of Currency Management

Forward Contract ★★

1. Adjust Hedge Ratios：Dynamic hedge →Rebalance

首先，持有外币 (FC) 头寸，如果 hedge → *Short FC forward=long DC forward*

- 方法一：定期对 hedge 本金的变化部分签新的合约 → 每 rebalance 一次，多一个合约。如果外币资产增值，需要 hedge 的更多，short 更多份的 FC forward（或 long 更多份 DC forward）
- 方法二：定期对原合约做反向头寸，并对新本金签订新合约 → 合约始终只有一份（FX Swap）

2. *Roll yield (short FC forward)= (F−S)/S* →

Roll yield =forward premium or discount

Roll yield will affect the cost/benefit analysis（相当于 hedge cost）

- *Positive* roll yield will shift the analysis *toward hedging*
- *Negative* roll yield will shift the analysis *away from hedging*

If the hedge requires：	$F_{P/B} > S_{P/B}$. $i_B < i_P$ Contango	$F_{P/B} < S_{P/B}$. $i_B > i_P$ Backwardation
A long forward	*Negative roll yield*, which increases hedging cost and discourages hedging	*Positive roll yield*，which decreases hedging cost and encourages hedging
A short forward	*Positive roll yield*，which decreases hedging cost and encourages hedging	*Negative roll yield*，which increases hedging cost and discourages hedging

Strategies to Modify Risk and Lower Hedging Costs ★★

GBP → USD：Hedge short exposure to the GBP

策略	特点
Forward contracts	• Expects the GBP to appreciate → *Reduce hedge ratio*，hedging less than the full exposure to GBP risk • Expects the GBP to depreciate → *Increase hedge ratio*，hedging more than the full exposure
Buy ATM put ★	• Asymmetric protection，eliminating all downside risk，retaining all upside potential • *Highest initial cost* but no opportunity cost
Buy OTM put ★	• Compared to buying ATM protective puts，this strategy *reduces the initial cost* of the hedge but does not eliminate all downside risk
Risk reversal or collar ★	• *Buy the lower cost 25-delta puts* on the GBP and *sell 25-delta calls* on the GBP • This strategy *further reduces initial cost* but also *limits upside potential* compared to buying out-of-the money put options only
Put spread ★	• *Buy OTM puts* on the GBP and *sell puts* that are further out of the money，(e.g.，buy a 35-delta put and sell a 25-delta put) • This strategy *reduces the initial cost* and also *reduces downside protection* compared to buying out-of-the money put options only
Seagull spread ★	• *Put spread combined selling a call* (e.g.，buy a 35-delta put，sell a 25-delta put，and sell a 35-delta call) • Compared to the put spread，only this hedge has *less initial cost* and the same down side protection，but *limits upside potential*
Exotic options	• Knock-in option，knock-out option，Binary or digital options

Hedging Multiple Currencies ★

1. 通常多币种组合不用 hedge → Consider *the correlation* between the various foreign-currency risk exposures
2. 决定 hedge
   - *Cross-hedges (proxy hedge)*：对 exposure being hedged 找替代
   - *Macro hedge*：Address portfolio-wide risk factors
   - *Minimum-variance hedge ratio (MVHR)*：

     $R_{DC} = 0.12+1.25(\%\Delta S_{USD/EUR}) + \varepsilon$ → *hedge ratio*=1.25

     $$h = \rho(R_{DC};\ R_{FX}) \times \left[\frac{\sigma(R_{DC})}{\sigma(R_{FC})}\right]$$

↓

Basis risk

Managing Emerging Market Currency

Two most important considerations

- *Higher trading costs than the major currencies* under normal market conditions
- *Increased likelihood of extreme market events* and *severe illiquidity* under stressed market conditions

Non-deliverable forwards (NDFs)

- 原因：Emerging market governments frequently *restrict delivery* of their currency and capital controls exist
- 表现：*Cash settlement* of gains or losses in a *developed market currency* → 计算

Reading 20

MARKET INDEXES AND BENCHMARKS

业绩归因、Equity 章节还有阐述

Benchmark Uses and Types

Valid benchmark 的特征

- Specified in advance
- Appropriate
- Measurable
- Unambiguous
- Reflective of current investment opinions
- Accountable
- Investable

Types of benchmarks

- Absolute return
- Manager universe
- Broad market index
- Investment style
- Factor-based models
- Return-based
- Custom

Index 的作用

- A reference point for portions of a sponsor's portfolio
- Communication between the plan sponsor and manager
- Communicating to others how to view manager
- Identification and evaluation of portfolio's risk exposures
- Interpretation of past performance
- Manager appraisal and selection
- Marketing of investment products
- Demonstration of compliance with regulations and laws

Index Weighting Schemes

优缺点

	Advantages	Disadvantages
Capitalization-Weighted	• *Requires less rebalancing* • Self-corrects for *stock splits*	• Overly influenced by *overpriced securities* • Overly concentrated， *less diversified*
Price-Weighted Index	• *Simplicity* of their construction • Has a *long historical track record*	• Overly *influenced by the highest-priced securities* • Do *not necessarily reflect the economic importance* • It *assumes an investor holds one unit* of each security • *Downward bias* in the index return (stock splits)
Equal-Weighted Indexes	• *Less concentrated in large-cap* securities and more diversified • *Provide an average* of all index security returns	• *Small-issuer bias* • *Increased liquidity problems* (inclusion of small issuers) • *Frequent rebalancing and high transaction* costs
Fundamental-Weighted Indexes	• Avoid the problem that Cap-weighted indexes overweight overvalued issues • *More representative of an issuer's importance in an economy*	• *Rely on subjective judgment* • *Less diversified than cap-weighted indexes* • Not all investors could hold a fundamental-weighted index because they are weighted by valuation metrics

Index 构建的考量因素 ★

Trade off	Details
Completeness vs. investability	✓ Completeness：Include *all securities* that meet benchmark criteria and provide complete coverage and *greater diversification* ✓ Investability：Inclusion of *smaller cap* and *less liquid* securities that are difficult or costly to purchase
Reconstitution and rebalancing (R&R) frequency vs. turnover	✓ Frequent R&R：Theoretically means the index *better reflects* the intended characteristics ● Reconstitution：The process of adding and deleting securities ● Rebalancing：Adjusting the weighting of existing securities in an index ✓ Turnover：Increased turnover and transaction *costs*
Objective and transparent(O&T) rules vs. judgment	✓ Rules：Changes to index is based on objective rules，allow those who *replicate or base holdings around the index* holdings to anticipate and plan for changes in the index，thus lowering the cost ✓ Judgment：In application of the rules to deal with changing or unanticipated situations

第 7 章

Fixed Income

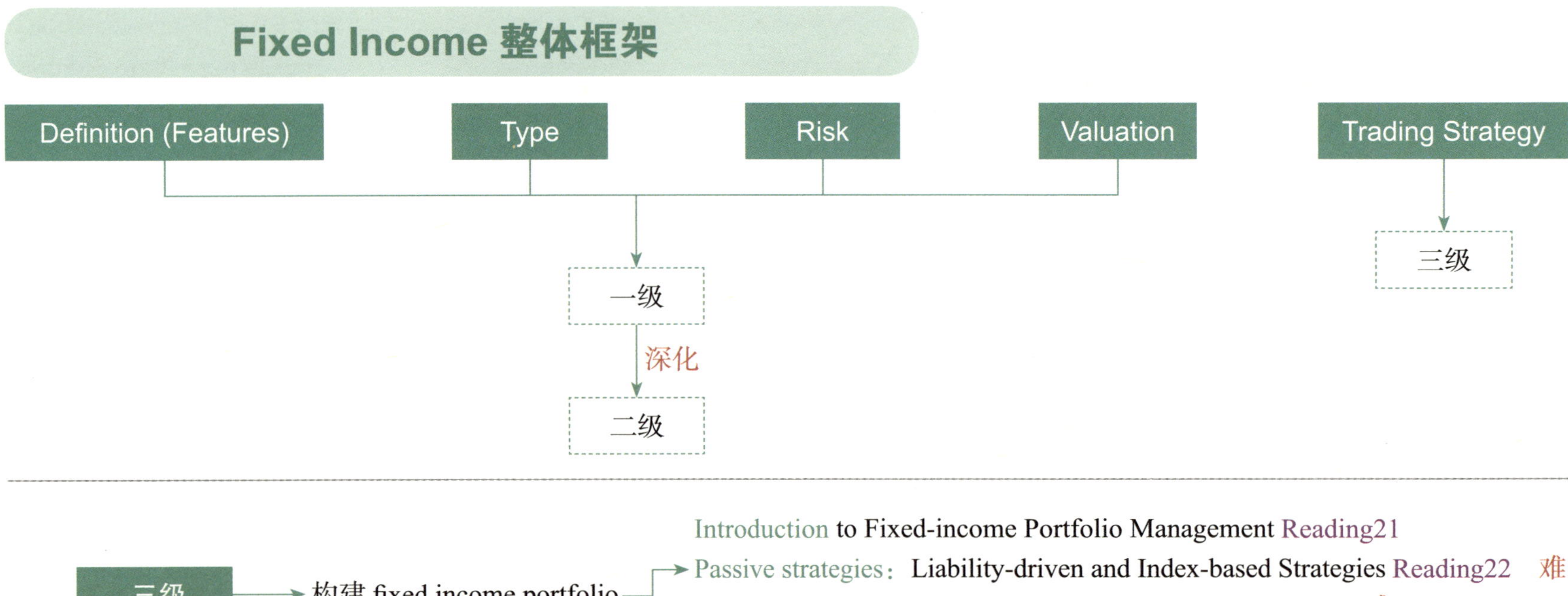

三级 → 构建 fixed income portfolio

- Introduction to Fixed-income Portfolio Management Reading21
- Passive strategies：Liability-driven and Index-based Strategies Reading22 难
- Active strategies
  - Yield Curve Strategies Reading23 难
  - Credit Strategies Reading24

Reading 21

INTRODUCTION TO FIXED-INCOME PORTFOLIO MANAGEMENT

Roles of Fixed-Income Securities in Portfolios ★★

结论

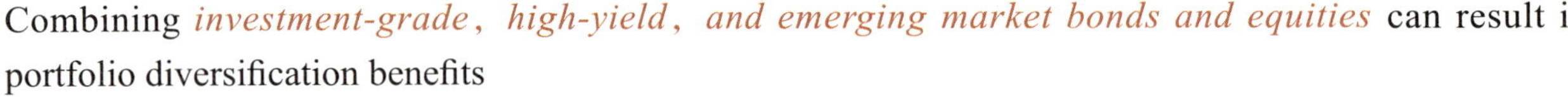

Diversification Benefits →

Combining *investment-grade, high-yield, and emerging market bonds and equities* can result in portfolio diversification benefits

- *Correlation* of returns between two asset classes are *not constant* over time
- *Volatility* of each asset class also affects portfolio risk

Benefits of Regular Cash Flows →

Regular cash flows allow individual and institutional investors to *meet predictable, and known future obligations (Liabilities)*

Inflation Hedging Potential →

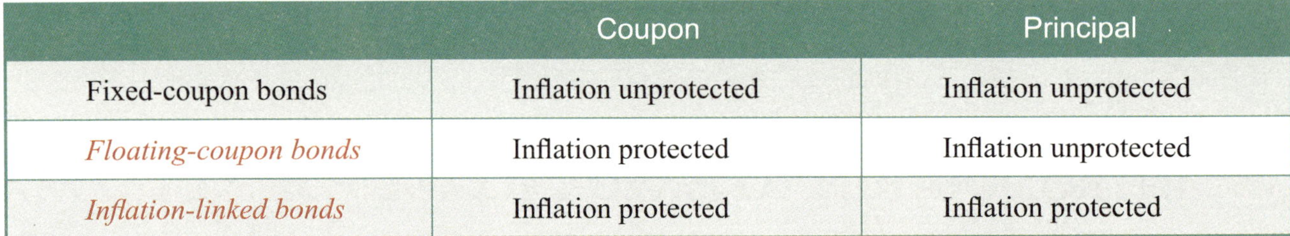

	Coupon	Principal
Fixed-coupon bonds	Inflation unprotected	Inflation unprotected
Floating-coupon bonds	Inflation protected	Inflation unprotected
Inflation-linked bonds	Inflation protected	Inflation protected

Fixed-Income Mandates

Liability-Based Mandates

计算、结论

Duration Matching ★★★

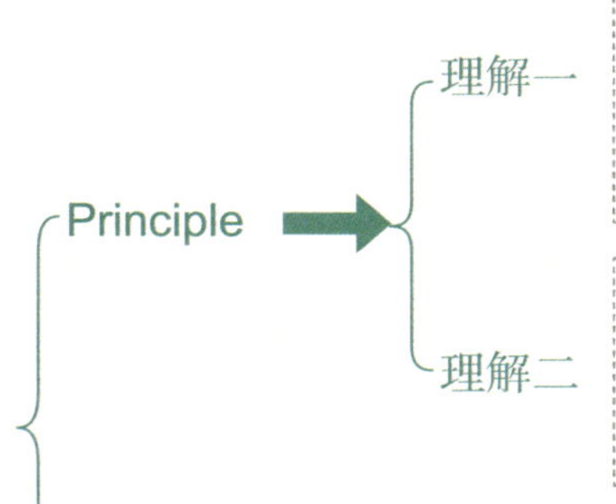

Principle — 理解一:

- *Changes in reinvestment income (reinvestment risk) and changes in bond prices (price risk) immunize* against the effect of interest rate changes
- *Minimize the variance in the realized rate of return* from the volatility of future interest rates over a known time horizon

Principle — 理解二:

"*Zero replication*": The performance of the bond portfolio over the investment horizon replicates the zero-coupon bond that provides for perfect immunization

- Zero-coupon bond: *No coupon reinvestment risk nor price risk*

Conditions:

- An initial *market value equals or exceeds the present value of the liability*
- *Portfolio Macaulay duration matches the liability's due date*
- *Minimizes the portfolio convexity* statistic

Portfolio Statistics 了解

- *Cash flow yield (an immunization strategy lock)*: *It is not the weighted average of the yields to maturity.* This difference between cash flow yield and yield to maturity arises *because of the steepness in the yield curve*
- *Macaulay duration*: *It is not the weighted average of duration*
- *Dispersion and convexity*: *Dispersion is the weighted variance of the times to receipt of cash flow. Assess the structural risk* to the interest rate immunization strategy

Considerations and Risks

结论

Structural risk (Immunization risk)	✓ *A sufficient, but not necessary,* condition for immunization is *a parallel shift* ✓ Structural risk: The risk is that *yield curve twists and non-parallel shifts* lead to changes in the cash flow yield that *do not match the zero-coupon bond* that provides for perfect immunization ● This risk is reduced by *minimizing the dispersion (minimizing the convexity)* of cash flows in the portfolio, going *from a barbell design to more of a bullet portfolio* ✓ *An exception would be zero-coupon bond: No price risk, no reinvestment risk,* and therefore *no immunization risk,* although credit risk remains
Rebalance	✓ *As market conditions change, the immunization conditions will be violated,* and the portfolio therefore needs to be *rebalanced periodically* ✓ The need to rebalance makes *liquidity considerations important* ✓ Immunization *assumes that bond issuers do not default* ✓ *If using bonds with embedded options,* a bond's duration is replaced by its *effective duration* as an input

Cash Flow Matching

How to Use Cash Flow Matching

计算★

Future liability payouts are exactly mirrored by *coupon and principal payments* arising from the bond portfolio

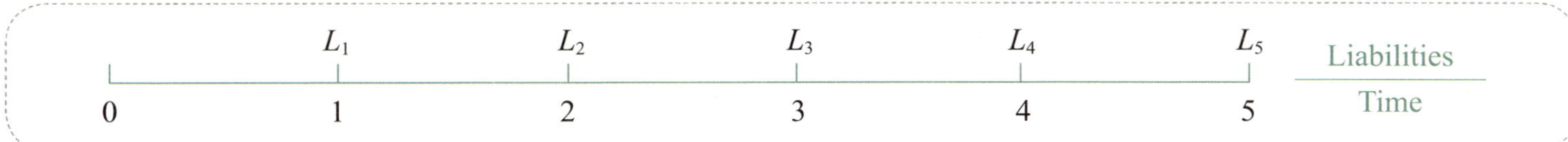

Step 1……

- Cash flow from Bond A selected to satisfy L_5
- $Coupons = A_c$; $Principal = A_p$ *and* $A_c + A_p = L_5$; Unfunded liabilities remaining:

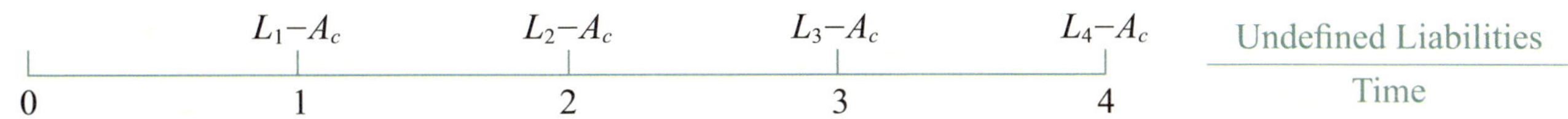

Advantages and Disadvantages

结论★

Advantages ➡

- The *simplest* and most *intuitive* way
- Unlike duration matching, *no underlying assumptions*
- In theory, *no need for reinvestment* of cash inflows and *no need for rebalance*
- A *motive* for cash flow matching can be *accounting defeasance*, whereby both the assets and liabilities are removed from the balance sheet

Disadvantages ➡

- Perfect matching of cash flows is difficult to achieve. Timing mismatches results in some *reinvestment risk*
- Implementing a cash flow matching approach may result in relatively *high transaction costs*
- A portfolio manager has an *incentive to rebalance the portfolio periodically*
- For some types of fixed-income securities， the *timing or amount* of cash flows may *change*

Key Features of Duration Matching，Cash Flow Matching and Tender Offer

- The *tender offer* entails buying the bonds at *higher price*. *Cash flow matching* entails buying even *more expensive government bonds*. The *duration matching* strategy can be implemented at a *lower cost*
- *Tender offer and cash flow matching* can *remove the debt liabilities* from the balance sheet， while under *duration matching*， the debt liabilities will *remain on the balance sheet*

	Duration Matching	Cash Flow Matching ★★★结论
Yield curve assumptions	*Parallel* yield curve shifts	None
Mechanism	Risk of shortfall is minimized by matching duration and present value of liabilities	Bond portfolio cash flows match liabilities cash flows
Basic principle	Cash flows come from *coupons and liquidating* bond portfolio positions offset liability cash flows	Cash flows come from *coupons and principal repayments* of the bond portfolio offset liability cash flows
Rebalancing	*Frequent rebalancing* required	*Not required* but often desirable
Complexity	High	Low
Cost	Low	High

Hybrid Approach ★★	
Contingent Immunization	✓ Combine *immunization with an active management* approach when the asset portfolio's value exceeds the present value of the liability portfolio ● *Active management*：Over-hedge or under-hedge the number of futures contracts ✓ If the actively managed portfolio value *falls to the specified threshold*，*active management ceases* and a conventional duration matching or a cash flow matching approach is put
Horizon Matching	✓ The *short-term* liability portion is covered by a *cash flow matching* approach ✓ The *long-term* liabilities are covered by a *duration matching* approach ✓ A portfolio manager has more flexibility over the less certain，longer horizon liabilities and can still meet more certain，shorter-term liabilities

结论

Total Return Mandates ★★★

结论

	Pure Indexing	Enhanced Indexing	Active Management
Characteristic	*Replicate* a bond index as closely as possible *difficult* and *costly* because bonds market are *illiquid*	Stratified *sampling* and *match primary risk factor (duration)*	Portfolio managers may *take views on portfolio duration that differ* from the benchmark
Objective	Match benchmark return and risk as closely as possible	Modest outperformance of benchmark while active risk is kept low	Higher outperformance of benchmark and higher active risk levels
Portfolio weights	Ideally *the same as benchmark* or only slight mismatch	*Small deviations* from underlying benchmark	*Significant deviations* from underlying benchmark
Risk factor matching	*Risk factors are matched exactly*	Most primary risk factors are closely matched (in particular, *duration*)	*Large risk factor deviations* from benchmark (in particular, duration)
Turnover	Similar to underlying benchmark	Slightly higher than underlying benchmark	Considerably *higher turnover* than the underlying benchmark
Return & risk	Targeted active return and active risk are both zero	Modest outperformance	*Significant return differences*
Management fee	Lowest	Modest	*Highest*

Bond Market Liquidity

Liquidity Differences among Bond Market Sub-Sectors  结论

- *Sovereign government bonds* are typically *more liquid*. Sovereign government bonds of countries with *high credit quality* are typically *more liquid* than bonds of lower-credit-quality countries
- Corporate bonds with *low credit quality have lower liquidity* than high credit
- Corporate bonds of *infrequent issuers* are often *less liquid*
- *Smaller issues* are generally *less liquid* than larger issues
- Bonds with *longer maturities* tend to be *less liquid* than nearer-term bonds
- Bond liquidity is typically *highest right after issuance (on-the-run issue)*

The Effects of Liquidity on Fixed-Income Portfolio Management 了解

Pricing → *less transparent*

- *Matrix pricing*

Portfolio Construction

- High *liquidity needs* → lower *yield*
- *Illiquidity* → *increases the cost of trading*
- *Conventional (plain vanilla)* corporate bonds normally have *lower spreads* than corporate bonds with *nonstandard or complex features*

Alternatives to Direct Investment in Bonds

✓ Fixed-income derivatives

✓ Fixed-income exchange-traded funds (ETFs) and pooled investment vehicles (such as mutual funds)

- Transact through in-kind deposits and redemptions

A Model for Fixed-Income Returns ★★★ 计算

$$E(R) \approx \textit{Yield income} + \textit{Rolldown return} + E\,(\textit{Change in price based on investor's views of yields and yield spread}) - E(\textit{Credit losses}) + E\,(\textit{Currency gains or losses})$$

Return Component	Description	Formula
Yield income	Coupon payments and reinvestment income	$\textit{Annual coupon payment} / \textit{Current bond price}$
+ *Rolldown return*	Bonds are pulled to par *as time to maturity decreases*	$\dfrac{\textit{Bond price}_{End} - \textit{Bond price}_{Beginning}}{\textit{Bond price}_{Beginning}}$
= *Rolling yield*		*Yield income* + *Rolldown return*
+ *E* (*Change in price based on yield and yield spread expectation*)	*Reflects an investor's expectation of changes in yields and yield spreads*	$[-MD \times \Delta yield] + \left[\frac{1}{2} \times Convexity \times (\Delta yield)^2\right]$
− *E* (*Credit losses*)	*PD*LGD*	Given
+ *E* (*Currency gains or losses*)		Given
= *Total expected return*		

Leverage in Fixed-Income Investment

Using Leverage 计算 ★★★

$$r_p=\frac{Portfolio\ return}{Portfolio\ equity}=\frac{[r_I\times(V_E+V_B)-(V_B\times r_B)]}{V_E}=r_I+\frac{V_B}{V_E}(r_I-r_B)$$

Risks of Leverage

- Leverage can lead to *forced liquidations ("fire sale")*
- During periods of *financial crisis*, *counterparties as lender* may *withdraw their financing*

Methods for Leveraging Fixed-Income Portfolios ★性质	
Futures contracts (explicit)	$Leverage_{Futures}=\frac{Notional\ value\ -\ Margin}{Margin}$
Swap agreements (explicit)	● *The fixed-rate payer is effectively short a fixed-rate bond and long a floating-rate bond* ● The *only capital required to enter into swap agreements is collateral*
Structured financial instruments (implicit)	● The inverse floater exacerbates the magnitude of inverse relationship between *P* and *r* ● The embedded leverage adds price volatility
Repurchase agreements (for the borrower's standpoint)	● From the standpoint of the *lender*, refer to as *reverse repos* ● *Cash-driven transactions*: One party that *owns bonds and wants to borrow cash*. They usually use *"general collateral"* ● *Security-driven transaction*: The lender typically seeks a *particular security* ● Bilateral repos or tri-party repos
Securities lending	● Motivation: *Short sales and financing/collateralized borrowing* ● Security lending transactions are *collateralized by cash or high-credit-quality bonds* ● Unlike repurchase agreements, security lending transactions are typically *open-ended*

Fixed-Income Portfolio Taxation

Key points for managing taxable fixed-income portfolios

✓ *Tax-loss harvesting*

✓ If *short-term capital gains tax rates are higher* than long-term capital gains tax rates，then be *prudential when realizing short term gains*

✓ Consider the *trade-off between capital gains and income* for tax purposes

✓ Example：*The taxation of capital gains and capital losses has minimal consequences to tax-exempt investors. Consistent with the portfolio manager's investment views*，the portfolio manager would likely liquidate Position A，which she considers slightly overvalued rather than liquidating Position B，which she considers slightly undervalued ★★★

从 tax 的角度考虑应该 liquidate 哪个 position？

Investment vehicles and taxes

✓ Pooled investment vehicle

- *Interest income*：For tax purposes the fund is considered to have distributed interest income for tax purposes in the year it is received
- *Taxation of capital gains*
  - *Pass-through treatment of capital gains*
  - *Deferral in capital gains tax payments*

✓ Separately managed account：Tax-loss harvesting

Reading 22

LIABILITY-DRIVEN AND INDEX-BASED STRATEGIES

Liability-Driven Investing

Asset-liability Management →

Liability-driven investing (LDI)：The liabilities are given and assets are managed

- Example：*A life insurance or pension*

Asset-driven liabilities (ADL)：The asset side results from underlying businesses

- Example：A *leasing company*

Classification of Liabilities ★★★判断

Liability Type	Amount of Cash Outlay	Timing of Cash Outlay	Example
I	Known	Known	*Traditional fixed-income bond having no embedded options*
II	Known	Uncertain	*Callable and putable bonds* *Term life insurance policy*
III	Uncertain	Known	*Floating-rate note* *Inflation-indexed bonds*
IV	Uncertain	Uncertain	*Property and casualty insurance companies DB pension plan*

Framework →
- Interest Rate Immunization—A Single liability　参考上一个 Reading 中的 Duration Matching 知识点
- Interest Rate Immunization—Multiple liabilities
- Liability-Driven Investing—An Example of DB Pension Plan

Interest Rate Immunization—Multiple Liabilities ★★★

- Cash Flow Matching ➡ 参考上一个 Reading 中的 Cash Flow Matching 知识点
- Duration Matching 结论 ➡
  - (1) *The market value of assets is greater than or equal to the market value of the liabilities*
  - (2) *The asset basis point value (BPV) equals the liability BPV*
  - (3) *The dispersion of cash flows and the convexity of assets are greater* than those of the liabilities
- Derivatives Overlay 计算 ➡
  - $Asset\ portfolio\ BPV + (N_f \times Futures\ BPV) = Liability\ portfolio\ BPV$
  - $Futures\ BPV \approx \frac{BPV_{CTD}}{CF_{CTD}}$, CF=Conversion factor
- Contingent Immunization ➡ 参考上一个 Reading 中 Contingent Immunization 知识点

Liability-Driven Investing—An Example of DB Pension Plan

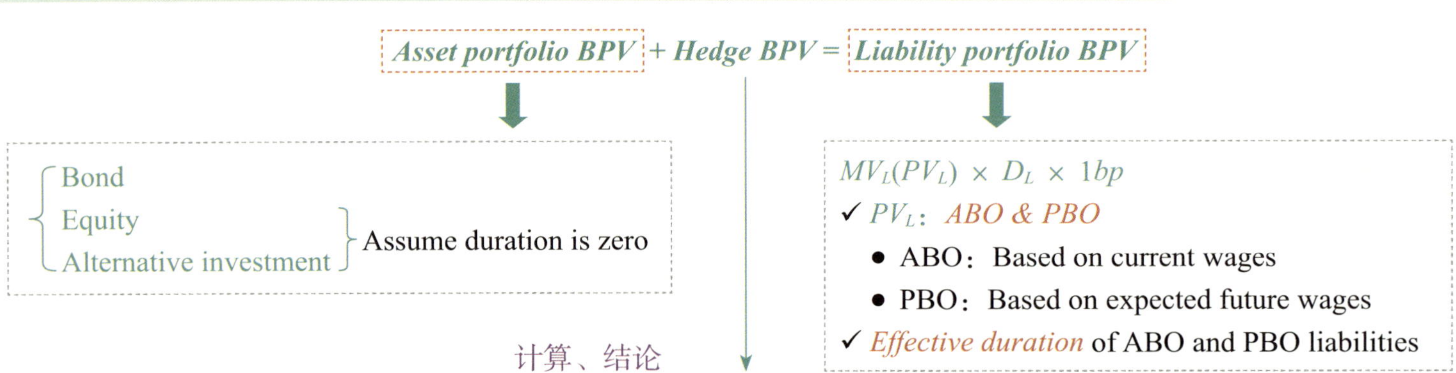

Managing the Duration Gap with Derivatives Overlay	
Futures	*Asset portfolio BPV* + N_f × *Futures BPV* = *Liability portfolio BPV*
Interest rate swap	$Asset\ BPV + [NP \times \frac{Swap\ BPV}{100}] = Liability\ BPV$ *Active management of the hedging ratio*： Lower rates → raise the hedging ratio
Swaption	*Negative* duration gap → long *receiver* swaption
Swaption collar	Combination of *buying receiver swaption and writing payer swaption*

The choice of derivatives overlay

- The swap rate to be *at or below current swap rate → receive-fixed swap*
- Swap rates are expected to be *above current swap rate → swaption collar*
- If rates are projected to reach a *certain threshold that depends on the option costs and the strike rates → receiver swaption*

Risks in Liability-Driven Investing ★★

结论

Asset BPV × Δ *Asset yields* + *Hedge BPV* × Δ *Hedge yields* ≈ *Liability BPV* × Δ *Liability yields*

Model risks	*Many assumptions* in the models and *approximations*. Examples ● DB：ABO or PBO；future events (e.g.，wage levels，time of retirement，and time of death) ● Approximate the asset portfolio duration using the weighted average of the individual durations → *A better approach is using the cash flow yield*
Spread risk	Assume *equal changes* in asset，liability，and hedging instrument yields (*ΔAsset Yields*，*ΔHedge Yields*，*and ΔLiability Yields*)
Counterparty credit risk	Uncollateralized interest rate swap
Collateral exhaustion risk	Available collateral becomes exhausted
Asset liquidity risk	Combine active investing to the otherwise passive fixed-income portfolios

Index-based Strategies

Advantages and the Challenges of Matching Index

Advantages

- ✓ *Mimic* the prevailing characteristics of the *overall* investments
- ✓ Consistent with the *efficient markets hypothesis*
- ✓ Investors have the ability to *gain broad exposure* to the fixed-income universe
- ✓ Possibility of greater *diversification*
- ✓ *Lower fees*: Low trading frequency and no requirement of in-depth analysis
- ✓ *Avoiding* the *downside risk* from active management

Challenges ★★ 结论

- ✓ The size and breadth of bond markets
  - Fixed-income markets are *larger* and *broader*
  - Full replication is *neither feasible nor cost-effective*
- ✓ *The wide array* of fixed-income security *characteristics*
- ✓ *Unique issuance and trading* patterns (*over-the-counter*)
- ✓ *Rebalancing* of bond market indexes occurs *frequently*

Benchmark Selection ★

选择一个适合的 index 作为 benchmark

需考虑的 factor ➡

- ✓ Selection is guided by the *specified goals and objectives* for the investment
  - *Degree of risk aversion* and *investment horizon*
- ✓ Fixed-income market dynamics can drive deviation from a stable benchmark
  - The finite maturity of bonds
  - Market dynamics and issuer preferences
  - "*Bums problem*": Value-weighted indexes → a *more leveraged issuer or sector to receive a higher weight*

Index-based Investments

Enhanced Indexing Strategy 结论

Primary indexing risk factors ★★★	
Interest rate risk (parallel)	*Small* parallel shift ✓ Portfolio duration：$D_P = w_1D_1 + w_2D_2 + w_3D_3 + \cdots + w_iD_i$ ✓ *Duration contribution* $= w_i \times D_i$ Large parallel changes：*Convexity adjustment*
Yield curve risk (non-parallel)	✓ Key rate duration ✓ PVD：*The proportion of the index's total duration* attributable to cash flows falling within the selected time periods
Spread risk	✓ *Spread duration*$_p$ → generally，$SD = D$ • Contribution to *SD* • Treasury bond 的 $SD = 0$ • Floating rate bond → $SD \neq D$ ✓ Match *sector and quality spread duration contribution*
Credit risk	*Percent in sector and quality*
Option risk	*Sector/coupon/maturity cell weights*

Enhancement strategies
• Lower cost enhancements • Issue selection enhancements • Yield curve enhancements • Sector/quality enhancements • Call exposure enhancements

Alternative Methods for Passive Bond Market Exposure ★★

性质对比

Methods	Characteristics
Mutual Funds	✓ Shares in mutual funds are *redeemable at the net asset value* with a one-day time lag ✓ *Economies of scale* for *smaller* investors ✓ *Increased diversification* ✓ The bond mutual fund has *no maturity date* ✓ *Redeem* holdings at the fund's *NAV rather than* facing a need to sell *illiquid* positions
Exchange-Traded Funds (ETF)	✓ *Trading on an exchange* ✓ Purchase or selling ETF shares to the fund *against a basket of underlying securities* ✓ *Greater bond ETF liquidity* versus mutual funds given their availability to be purchased or sold *throughout the trading day* at a discount or premium relative to the NAV ● The *divergence to persist*
Synthetic Strategies (Total Return Swap)	*Total return reciever* ← *Index CF + Appreciation* — *Total return payer* *Total return reciever* → *LIBOR + Spread* / *Index depreciation + Default Losses* → *Total return payer* ✓ It requires *less initial cash outlay* ✓ TRS can *offer exposure to assets that are difficult to access directly* ✓ A TRS carries *counterparty credit risk*, *rollover risk* and require *greater regulatory oversight*

Laddered Bond Portfolio

Laddared Portfolio	Bullet Portfolio	Barbell Portfolio
Spread the bonds' maturity and par values evenly along the yield curve	Concentrates the bonds at a particular point on the yield curve	Place the bonds at the short-term and long-term ends of the curve

Advantages of the laddered portfolio ★★★结论

- *Yield curve diversification.* By spreading out the maturities in the ladder formation, the portfolio has the benefit of diversification
- *Liquidity management.* As time passes, there is always a bond that is close to redemption
- *Convexity.* If the three portfolios have the same duration (and cash flow yield), then the barbell clearly has the highest convexity and the bullet the lowest

Reading 23

YIELD CURVE STRATEGIES

Foundational Concepts for Yield Curve Strategies ★

结论

A Review of Yield Curve Dynamics ★★	
Level	A *parallel shift* in the yield
Slope	*Spread = Yield on a long-maturity bond − the yield on a shorter-maturity bond* ● *Flattening* (spread narrows) or *steepening* (spread widens)
Curvature	*Butterfly spread = −(Short-term yield) + (2× Mid-term yield) − (Long-term yield)* ● *Larger* butterfly spread → *more curvature*

Duration Measures

✓ Macaulay duration

✓ Modified duration

✓ Effective duration

✓ Money duration (dollar duration)

- *Money duration = Market value × modified duration*

✓ *PVBP = Market value × modified duration/10 000*

✓ Key rate duration (partial duration)

Convexity

✓ The *expected return* of a bond with higher-convexity *will be higher* than an identical-duration, *lower-convexity* bond *if interest rates change*

✓ A bond with *higher convexity* might be expected to have a *lower yield*

✓ The *more widely dispersed a bond's cash flows* are around the duration point, *the more convexity* it will exhibit

✓ *Negative convexity*

- Bonds with *short options* positions embedded (such as MBS or callable bonds)

Major Types of Yield Curve Strategies

Strategies Under a Stable Yield Curve 结论

1. Buy and Hold ➡ Position the portfolio with *longer duration and higher yield to maturity*

2. Riding the Yield Curve ★★★

条件	*Stable and upward-sloping* yield curve
做法	Purchase bonds with *maturities longer than his investment horizon* ✓ As the bond approaches maturity (i.e., *rolls down the yield curve*), it is valued using successively *lower yields and, therefore, at successively higher prices* ✓ particularly *effective* with *relatively steep yield curve*
对比 buy-and-hold	*Similarity*: Once purchased, are not typically traded *Difference*: ✓ *Expected accumulation*: Add to returns by *selling the security at a lower yield* at the horizon ✓ *Time horizon*: Four year investment horizon ● Buy-and-hold: Buy bond with *four-year* maturity ● Riding the Yield Curve: Buy bond with *five-year* maturity, then *selling in the fourth year*

3. Sell Convexity ★★★

Principle	*Sell convexity and earn additional returns*
How	● *Sell calls* on bonds held in the portfolio, or *sell puts* on bonds he would be willing to own ● *Buying securities with negative convexity*, such as callable bonds or MBS

4. Carry Trade

Buying a security and financing it at a rate that is lower than the yield on that security

Strategies for Changes in Level，Slope，or Curvature

1. Duration Management

Principle	*Rising* interest rates → *shortens* portfolio duration *Declining* interest rates → *lengthens* portfolio duration 结论
Duration Positioning	The "best" bond：$Total\ return \approx -1 \times Effective\ duration_E \times (YTM_E - YTM_B) + YTM_B$
Alter Portfolio Duration 计算	*Using futures contracts* $Number\ of\ contracts\ required = \frac{Required\ additional\ PVBP}{PVBP\ of\ the\ futures\ contract}$ *Using Interest rate swaps*：*PVBP of a receive-fixed swap = PVBP of a fixed-rate bond − PVBP of a floating-rate bond* • *Receive-fixed swap* can *increase* duration. *Fixed Paying* can *decrease* duration *Using leverage* • *Additional MV to be purchased using leverage* = *Required additional PVBP/Duration of bonds* × 10 000 • Calculate the *effective portfolio duration*：$\frac{Notional\ portfolio\ value}{Portfolio\ equity} \times Duration$ • *Advantage*：Leverage alone can perform the duration extension—there is no need to use longer-duration bonds • *Disadvantage*：Leverage adds *interest rate risk*，also increase *credit risk and liquidity risk*

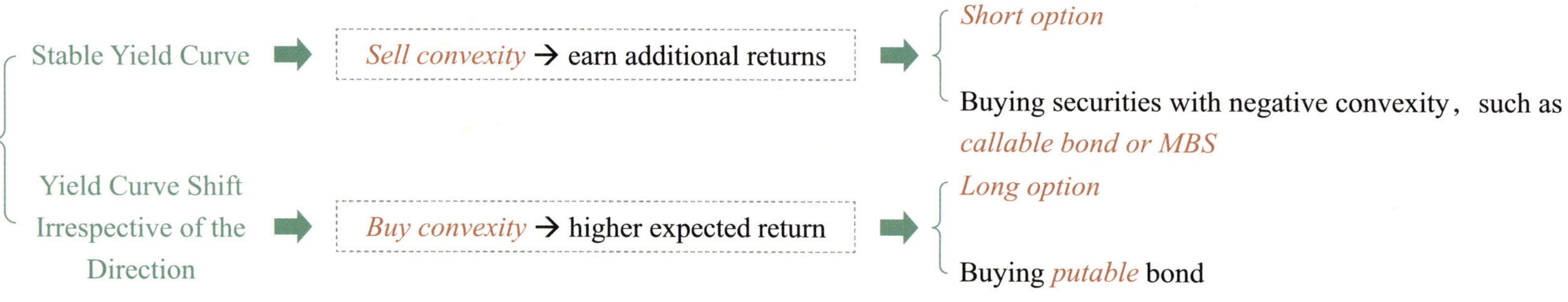

Changing Convexity	
Using Options	**Using Securities with Embedded Options**
• *Adding convexity is equivalent to add more curvature* to the price—yield function • The dynamic of the *rapid change in delta* is the essence of *convexity* • For the portfolio to benefit from higher convexity, the anticipated decline in rates must occur within a *short window of time* • There is *the drag on performance created by owning convexity when interest rates do not move up or down*	• The *yield advantage* of MBS or callable bond boosts returns in scenarios where there is little change in rates

3. Bullets and Barbells & Butterflies and Condors ★★★ 结论

Yield Curve Scenario		Barbell	Bullet
Level change	Parallel shift	Outperforms	Underperforms
Slope change	Flattening	Outperforms	Underperforms
	Steepening	Underperforms	Outperforms
Curvature change	Less curvature	Underperforms	Outperforms
	More curvature	Outperforms	Underperforms
Rate volatility change	Decreased rate volatility	Underperforms	Outperforms
	Increased rate volatility	Outperforms	Underperforms

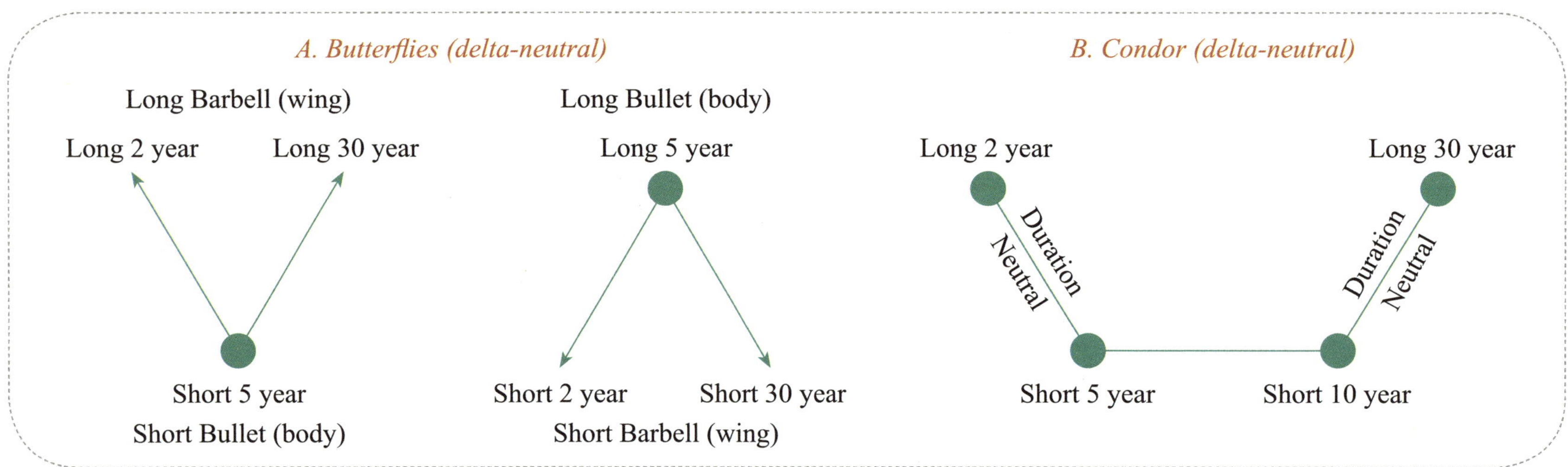

Yield Curve Scenario		Butterflies	Condor
Level change	Parallel shift	Long wing，short body	Long wing，short body
Slope change	Flattening	Long wing，short body	Long wing，short body
	Steepening	Long body，short wing	Long body，short wing
Curvature change	Less curvature	Long body，short wing	Long body，short wing
	More curvature	Long wing，short body	Long wing，short body
Rate volatility change	Decreased rate volatility	Long body，short wing	Long body，short wing
	Increased rate volatility	Long wing，short body	Long wing，short body

A Framework for Evaluating Yield Curve Trades ★ 同 "A Model for Fixed-Income Returns"

$$E(R) \approx Yield\ income + Rolldown\ return + E(Change\ in\ price\ based\ on\ investor's\ views\ of\ yields\ and\ yield\ spread) - E(Credit\ losses) + E(Currency\ gains\ or\ losses)$$

Return Component	Description	Formula
Yield income	Coupon payments and reinvestment income	$Annual\ coupon\ payment / Current\ bond\ price$
+ *Rolldown return*	Bonds are pulled to par *as time to maturity decreases*	$\frac{Bond\ price_{End} - Bond\ price_{Beginning}}{Bond\ price_{Beginning}}$
= *Rolling yield*		*Yield income + Rolldown return*
+ *E (Change in price based on yield and yield spread expectation)*	*Reflects an investor's expectation of changes in yields and yield spreads*	$[-MD \times \Delta yield] + \left[\frac{1}{2} \times Convexity \times (\Delta yield)^2\right]$
− *E (Credit losses)*	*PD*LGD*	Given
+ *E (Currency gains or losses)*		Given
= *Total expected return*		

Reading 24

FIXED-INCOME ACTIVE MANAGEMENT：CREDIT STRATEGIES

Investment-Grade & High-Yield Corporate Bond Portfolio

Risk	结论
Credit Risk	● *Credit loss rate = Default rate × loss severity* ● *Credit loss rates are much higher for high-yield bonds*. So *credit risk* is the most important consideration for *high-yield* portfolio. For *investment-grade* portfolio managers, *interest rate risk*, *spread risk*, *and credit migration risk* are typically the most relevant considerations
Credit Migration Risk and Spread Risk	*Spread duration* ● *Non-callable*, *fixed-rate* corporate bonds → $SD = D$ ● *Floating-rate* bonds (floaters) → $SD \neq D$ *Investment-Grade & High-Yield Corporate Bond* ● Investment-grade bonds: *Credit spread volatility* is more relevant ● High-yield bonds: Emphasis on *credit risk and market value* of the position
Interest Rate Risk	IGB have *more exposure to interest rate risk* than HYB ● Credit spreads is *negatively correlated* with risk-free interest rates *Empirical duration* ● Run a *regression of its price returns on changes in a benchmark interest rate* ● Empirical duration is *smaller* than the theoretically based effective duration ● The *difference between effective & empirical duration* is *largest for HYB*
Liquidity and Trading	● *Investment-grade* issues are, on average, *more liquid* than high-yield issues ● *Bonds are quoted differs*: *Investment-grade* bonds → *Spreads* over benchmark; *High-yield* bonds → *Price terms*

Credit Spreads  结论

Credit Spread Measures

Credit Spread	Calculation	Key Advantages
Benchmark Spread and G-Spread	$Benchmark\ spread = Yield_{bond} - Yield_{benchmark\ bond}$ $G\text{-}Spread = Y_{bond} - Y_{government\ bond}$ 计算 ● *On-the-run and duration match*	● An investor can hedge the interest rate risk of a credit security by *selling the duration-weighted amounts of the two benchmark government bonds* ● Useful for *estimating yield and price changes*
I-Spread	$I\text{-}Spread = Y_{bond} - Swap\ rate$	● Swap curves may be *"smoother"*
Z-Spread and OAS	$P_{market} = \frac{C}{(1+S_1+Z)^1} + \frac{C+prin}{(1+S_2+Z)^2}$ $P_{market} = \frac{CF_1}{(1+S_1+OAS)^1} + \frac{CF_2}{(1+S_2+OAS)^2}$	● *Option-adjusted spread (OAS)* is most useful for comparing bonds with *different features*, *such as embedded options* ● Z-spread and OAS used to *compare relative value* across credit securities ● *Benchmark spread*, the G-spread, and the I-spread are particularly useful for *pricing and hedging* credit securities

Excess Return ➡ $EXP \approx (s \times t) - (\Delta s \times SD) - (t \times p \times L)$

★★★计算

Credit Strategy Approaches

 结论

Bottom-Up Approach

- *Assess the relative value of individual bonds or issuers.* The investor has *conducted extensive research on companies* within the industries

Top-Down Approach

- *First determine which sectors have attractive relative value and then selects bonds within those sectors.* Top-down approach involves taking views on *macro factors*

The Bottom-Up Approach

Dividing the Credit Universe

- *Company-level risks*, rather than industry or macro risks, to be the dominant factors within each sector

Bottom-Up Relative Value Analysis

Weighing the *compensation for credit-related risks* (EXR) *against the credit-related risks*

- *Analyze excess return*: $EXR \approx (s \times t) - (\Delta s \times SD) - (t \times p \times L)$
- *Liquidity, portfolio diversification, and risk* are all important considerations
- *Spread curves* analysis
- *Bond structure*: *Subordinated debt* offers *more* credit spread than senior debt *Callable debt* has a *larger OAS* than comparable non-callable debt
- *Issuance date*: *Recently issues* tend to have *narrower bid-offer spreads*
- *Supply*: *New issue → Spreads widen*

Bottom-Up Portfolio Construction

- Market value or spread duration

The Top-Down Approach

Credit Quality	• *Credit spreads narrow* and default rates are lower or declining → *more low-quality bonds*; *credit spreads widen* and default rates are higher or rising → *higher-quality bond* • Measuring Credit Quality: Average credit rating (*non-arithmetic* weightings); *Duration Times Spread* (DTS)
Industry Sector Allocation	• Base on a portfolio *manager's macro views* • Compare the *average spread* of bonds within an individual industry sector and rating category
Interest Rate Measurement and Management	• In *bottom-up* approach, try to *mitigate the interest rate exposure* • In *top-down* approach, *actively manage the portfolio based on expectations of future changes in interest rates* and future interest rate volatility
Country and Currency Exposure	• Portfolio managers can benefit from higher return potential but may also be subject to additional risk
Spread Curves	• Spread curves can be constructed for a larger credit segment, such as an industry, currency, or index, in a top-down approach

ESG Considerations in Credit Portfolio Management

- *Relative value considerations*: Companies and industries with poor ESG practices may have more credit risk
- *Guideline constraints*
- *Portfolio-level risk measures*: Monitoring of exposures to ESG-related risk factors
- *Positive impact investing opportunities*

Liquidity Risk and Tail Risk in Credit Portfolios

Liquidity Risk	
Measures ★★★结论	• *Trading Volume*：The reduction of holdings decreased liquidity • *Spread Sensitivity to Fund Outflows*：*Less* spread sensitivity to fund outflows→liquidity *increases* • *Bid-Ask Spreads*：More-volatile market conditions have a negative effect on bid-ask spreads
Structural Industry Changes	Following the crisis，the cost of capital for dealers increased substantially，and the ability and willingness of dealers to maintain large bond positions decreased significantly
Management	Cash，more-liquid credit securities，liquid，non-benchmark bonds，CDS derivatives and ETFs
Tail Risk	
Assess ★★★结论	*Scenario Analysis*：Historical and hypothetical scenario analysis • *Correlations in Scenario Analysis*：During *financial crisis*，correlations tend to move closer to *1.0*
Management	• Portfolio Diversification • Tail Risk Hedges：Use securities or derivatives that act as "insurance"，such as *CDS and options*

International Credit Portfolios ★★ 结论

Relative Value in International Credit Portfolios

- *Credit cycles* typically affect the entire global credit universe，but to *varying degrees* across regions
- The *credit quality* of issuers typically differs by region
- *Sector composition* also differs by region
- Market factors，including both *supply and demand* factors，often vary globally with respect to corporate bonds
- *The US credit market is one of the most liquid*，emerging markets tend to be illiquid
- Currency risk in Global Credit Portfolios：Hedge currency risk → using *currency swaps or investing Pegged (or tightly managed) currencies*
- *Legal Risk*：Global differences in regulations and laws

Differences between Emerging & Developed Market

- *Concentration in commodities and banking*：*Commodity producers and banks represent a much higher proportion* of emerging market indexes
- *Government ownership*：Historically，*recovery rates* for emerging market bonds in default are *lower* than in developed markets
- *Credit quality*：Emerging market credit universe has a *high concentration* in both the *lower portion of the investment-grade rating* spectrum and the *upper portion of high yield*

Structured Financial Instruments

结论

Benefit from using structured financial instruments

- Higher portfolio *returns*
- Relative value opportunities: Exposure of *real estate*, *interest rate volatility*, *or consumer credit*
- *Improved portfolio diversification*

Type	Advantages
MBS	✓ Liquidity, exposure to real estate, exposure to expected changes in interest rate volatility ✓ Base on views of the credit cycle and the real estate cycle
ABS	Provide a way for investors to express views on *consumer credit*
CDO	✓ *Relative Value.* The valuation of CDOs may vary from the valuation of their underlying collateral ✓ *Exposure to Default Correlations* ● As *correlations increase*, *the value of mezzanine tranches usually increases* relative to the value of senior and equity tranches ● If an investor expects the default *correlation* to be substantially *negative*, she can try to profit by *selling the subordinated tranche*, *and buying the senior tranche* ● If the investor expects the *correlation* to be highly *positive*, she can try to profit by *selling (or selling short) senior tranche and buying subordinated tranche* ✓ *Leveraged Exposure to Credit.* Mezzanine and equity tranches
Covered Bonds	Because of this *dual protection* for creditors, covered bonds usually carry *lower credit* risks and *offer lower yields*

第 8 章

Equity Management

Reading 25

EQUITY PORTFOLIO MANAGEMENT

Equity Portfolio Management

Approaches to Equity Investment

Passive management

- Market is efficient
- Research will not provide sufficient return to cover cost

Active management

- Inefficient market
- Research will lead to outperform the market net of all coasts

Semi-active management

- Between
- Extract information not in stock prices with limited tracking risks

IR 比较 → *IR*：passive < active < semi-active

➢ 3 types of approaches vs. *IPS factors*

Factors	Approach
Tax (others)	Low turnover—fewer capital gains recognized
Large cap	More probably efficient—passive
Small cap	Although more mispricing—high transaction cost for active
International market	Lack of information—passive ok

Passive Investment

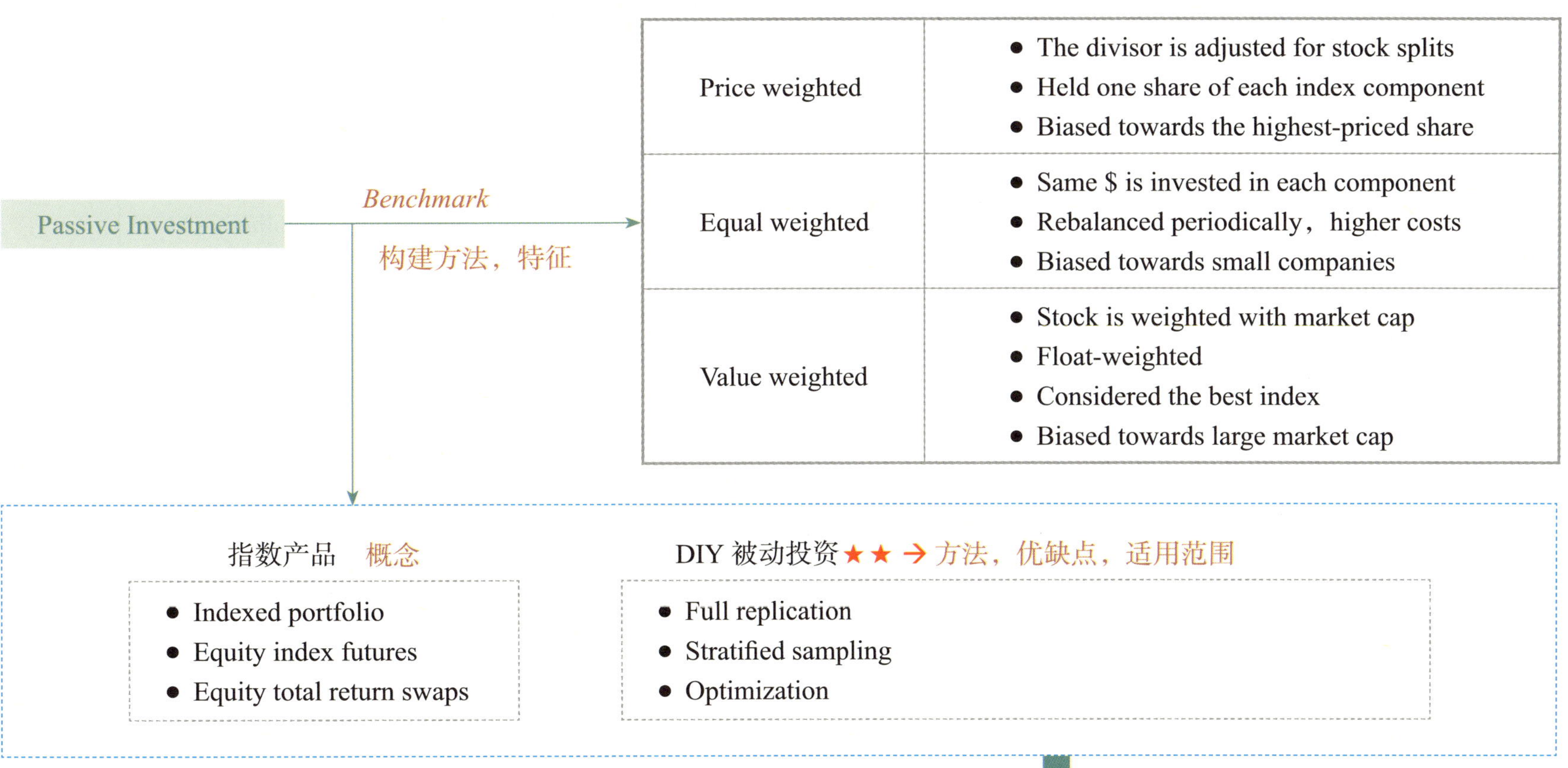

ETF vs. Mutual Fund

	ETF	Conventional index mutual funds
Frequently traded	More	Less
Shareholder record keeping costs	No	Yes
License fees	Higher	Lower
Tax efficient	More	Less
Cost for long term investor	Lower	Higher

DIY 被动投资

Passive investment	Suitable for	Advantage
Full Replication	• Smaller indices • Index stocks are liquid • More funds to invest	• Low tracking risk • Only rebalanced when the index stocks change or pay dividends
Stratified Sampling	• Large numbers of stocks are in the index • The stocks are illiquid	• Can mimic the performance without taking actual concentrated positions
Optimization	• Large numbers of stocks are in the index • The stocks are illiquid	• Lower tracking risk than stratified sampling

Active Investment

Classification of Equity Style

Styles from Character dimension

Style	Substyle
Value	• High Dividend Yield • Low *P/E* or *P/B* • Contrarian
Growth	• Consistent growth • Earning momentum
Market-oriented	• Market-oriented with a value bias • Market-oriented with a growth bias • Growth at a reasonable price (GARP) • Style rotators

Styles from size dimension

- Micro-cap
- Small-cap
- Mid-cap
- Large-cap

识别

Return-based style analysis

The indices → mutually exclusive, exhaustive, and represent distinct, uncorrelated sources of risk
The coefficient of determination → style fit
An error term → selection return

Holding-based style analysis 方法、比较、优缺点

Attributes	Value-oriented	Growth-oriented
Valuation levels	• Low price multiples • High dividend	• High price multiples • Low dividend
EPS growth rate	• Lower	• Higher, increasing • Low dividend
Earnings variability	• Greater	• Smaller
Industry sector	• Finance, utilities	• Technology, healthcare

	Advantages	Disadvantages
Return-based	● Characterizes entire portfolio ● Facilitates comparisons of portfolios ● Aggregates the effect of the investment process ● Different models usually give broadly similar results and portfolio characterizations ● Clear theoretical basis for portfolio categorization ● Requires minimal information ● Can be executed quickly ● Cost effective	● May be ineffective in characterizing current style ● Error in specifying indices in the model may lead to inaccurate conclusions
Holding-based	● Characterizes each position ● Facilitates comparisons of individual positions ● In looking at present，may capture changes in style more quickly than returns-based analysis	● Does not reflect the way many portfolio managers approach security selection ● Requires specification of classification attributes for style；different specifications may give different results ● More data intensive than returns-based analysis

Style drift

- Not receive the desired style exposure
- Drift from their area of expertise

SRI

- Bias towards small-cap and growth stocks

Long-short Investing

Basic Characteristic

- ➢ *Two alphas*
- ➢ *Symmetric distribution* of active weights
- ➢ The strategy is portable
- ➢ *Pair trade* with *company specific risk*
- ➢ High *leverage*

Price Inefficiency on the Short Side

- ➢ Few search for overvalued stocks
- ➢ Management promote the firm's stock
- ➢ Analysts are more likely to issue buy recommendations than sell recommendations
- ➢ And the pressure analysts face from management against issuing sell recommendations

Short 易得 alpha 原因

方法★

Equitizing a Market Neutral Long-short Portfolio

- Holding a permanent stock index futures position
- Long-short stocks to gain alpha

Short Extension Strategy → 120/20

- Equity strategy， not alternative investment
- Better exploit information
- Frees up additional funds
- Can be implemented without a derivatives market
- Coordinated portfolio

Selling Discipline

- ✓ Strategy of substitution
- ✓ Deteriorating fundamentals sell discipline
- ✓ Other selling disciplines will be based on rules
  - Valuation-level sell discipline
  - Down-from-cost sell discipline
  - Up-from-cost sell discipline
  - Target price sell discipline

Semi-active Equity Investing

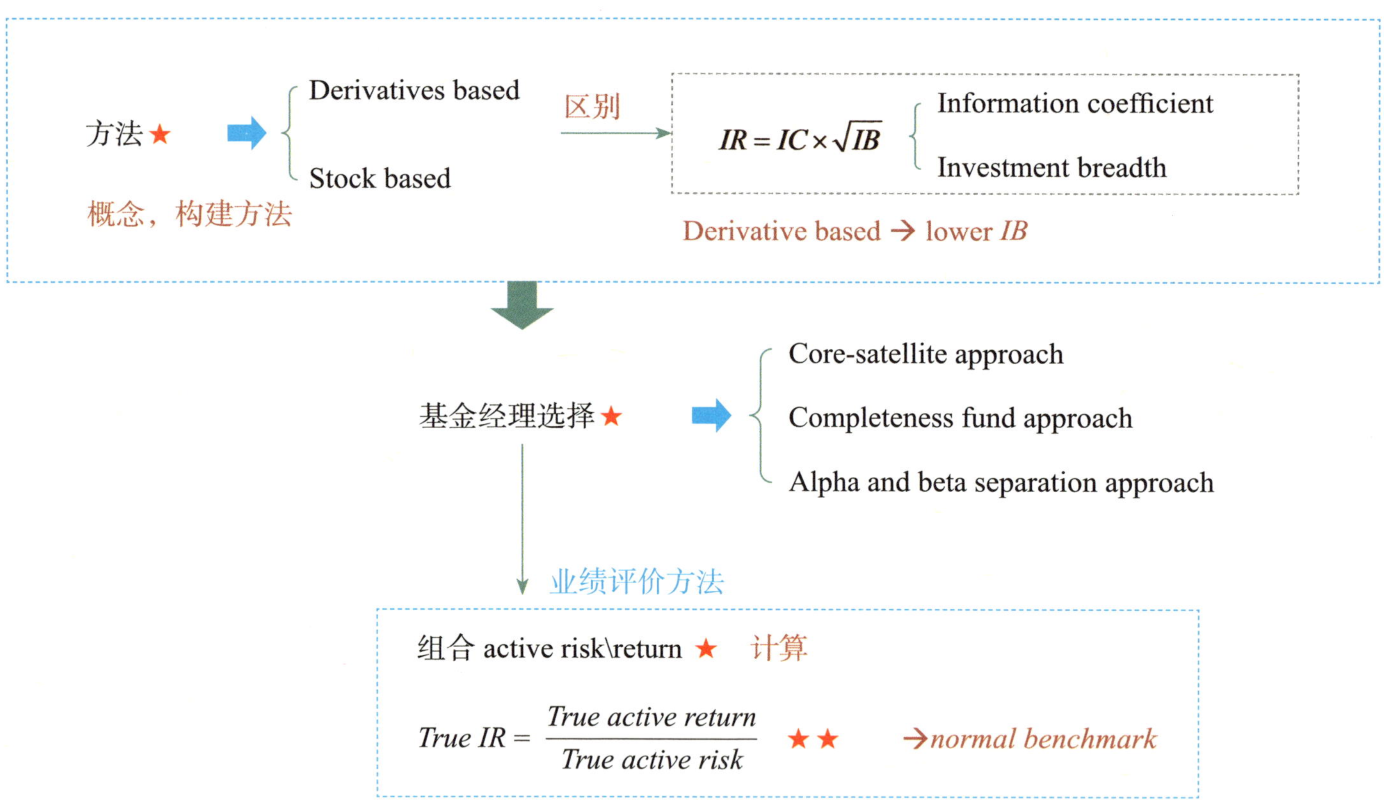

第 9 章

Alternative Management

Reading 26

ALTERNATIVE INVESTMENTS PORTFOLIO MANAGEMENT

Alternative Investment Groups

Reasons for investing 

- ➢ Risk diversification
- ➢ Active management
- ➢ Both of above

Common features

- ➢ Low liquidity
- ➢ Diversifying potential
- ➢ High DD costs
- ➢ Difficult performance evaluation
- ➢ Informationally less efficient

Issues for private wealth clients ★

- ➢ Taxes
- ➢ Suitability (time horizon, liquidity needs, emotional needs)
- ➢ Communication with client
- ➢ *Decision risk* ★
- ➢ Concentrated position

Classification

1. By traditional-or-modern distinction

Traditional Alternative	Modern Alternative	Traditional Investment
• Private Equity • Commodities • Real Estate	• Hedge Fund • Managed Futures • Distressed Securities	• Stocks • Bonds

2. By the primary role they usually play in portfolios

- ➢ Risk factors not easily accessible through traditional stock and bond investments → *Real estate* and (*long-only*) *commodities*
- ➢ Specialized investment strategies run by an outside manager → *Hedge funds and managed futures*
- ➢ Combine features of the prior two groups → *PE funds* and *distressed securities*

Real Estate

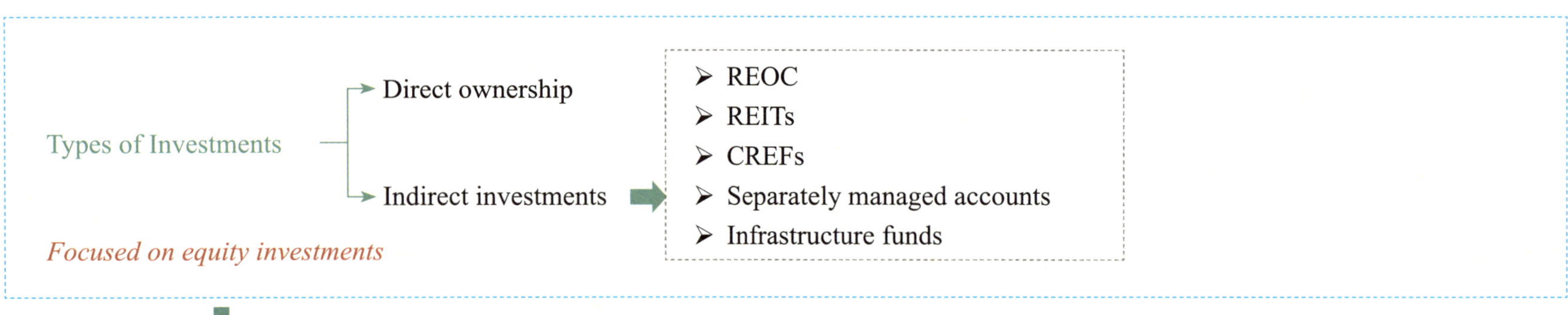

Investment Characteristics ★

- Total return
- Relative lack of liquidity
- Large lot sizes
- Relatively high transaction costs
- Heterogeneity
- Immobility
- Low information transparency
- The lack of reliable data
- Various factors affect D&S
- Mixed inflation-hedging effect
- Idiosyncratic risk

直接投资优缺点★

Advantage

- Tax deductible expense
- Ability to use leverage
- More direct control
- Diversify geographically
- Lower volatility of returns

Disadvantage

- Not dividable，large idiosyncratic risks
- High information cost
- High transaction and operating costs
- Special geographical risks
- Political risks

Benchmark ★★

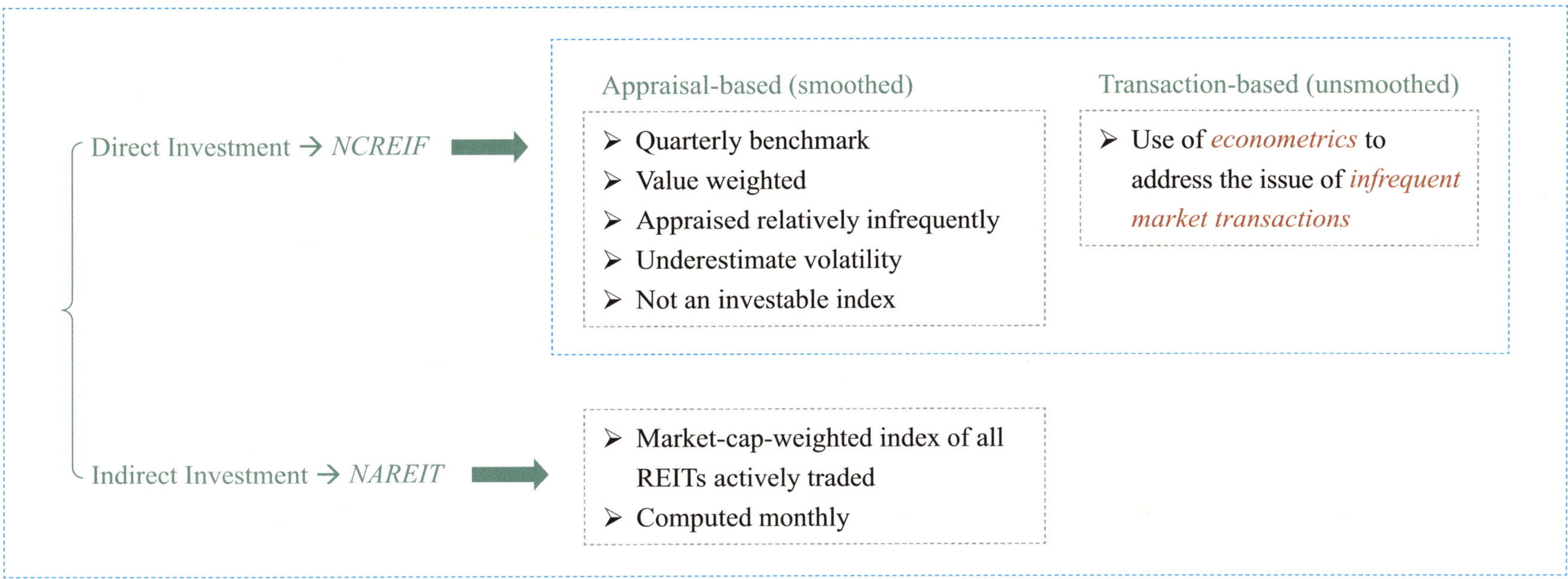

Historical Performance 了解

Private Equity

Definition

- Capital is raised via a private placement
- Unregulated
- Institute investors

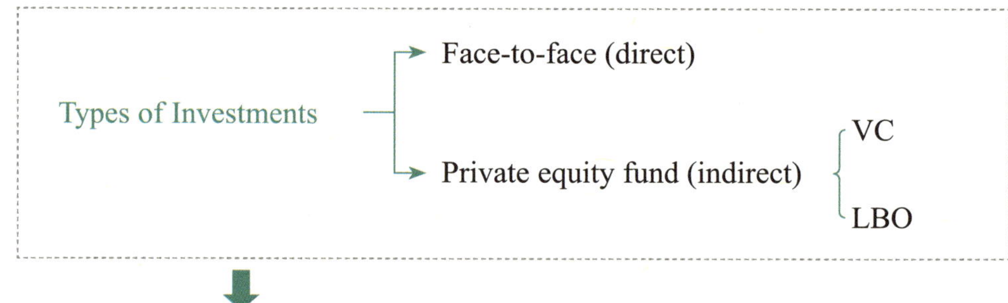

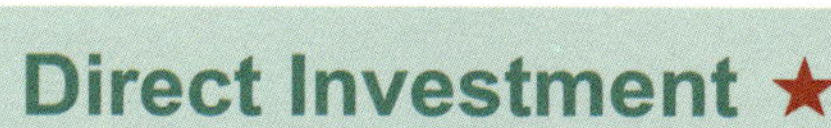

Private Equity Investments	Publicly Traded Securities
Deal structure and price are *negotiated*	Price is set in the *context* of the *market*
Investor can *request access to all information*	Analysts can use *only publicly available* information
Investors *heavily involved*	*Limited access to management*

投资方法

Convertible Preferred Stock

- Must be paid a *specified amount before common shareholder*
- *More valuable than those issued earlier*
- Common equity at a favorable price will *trigger conversion*

Indirect Investment ★★

Limited Partnership → GP&LP

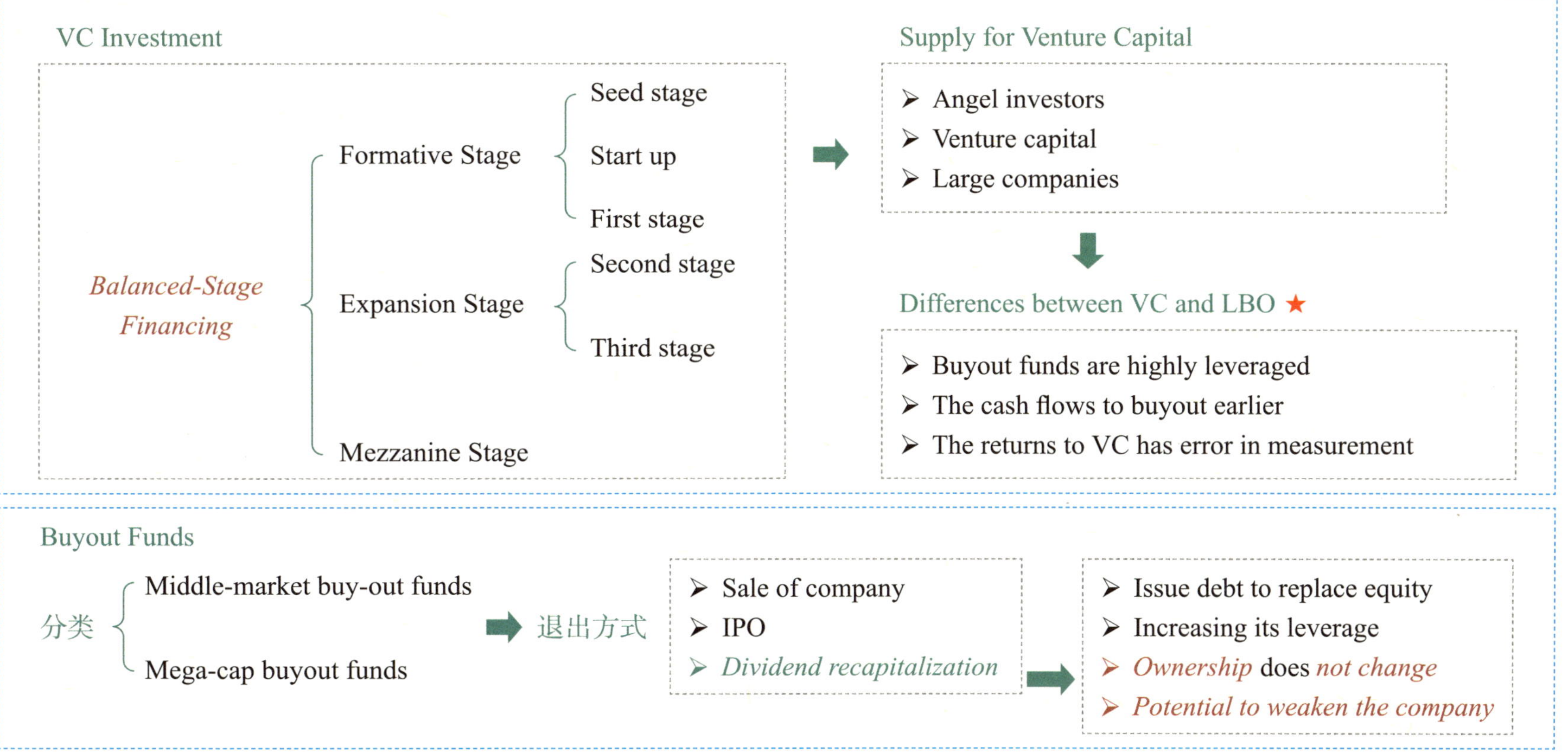

Practical Issues

Limited Partnership

LP —fee→ GP

➢ Management fee
- Based upon the *committed fund*
- *May decline* over time

➢ Carried interest (*2-20*)
- *Hurdle rate*
- *Claw-back provision*

Historical Performance 了解

Investment Characteristics ★

- Illiquidity
- Long-term commitments required
- Higher risk
- Higher *IRR* required
- Limited information (VC only)

Roles in Portfolios

- Ability to achieve sufficient diversification
- Low liquidity of the position
- Provision for capital commitment
- Appropriate diversification strategy

Commodity

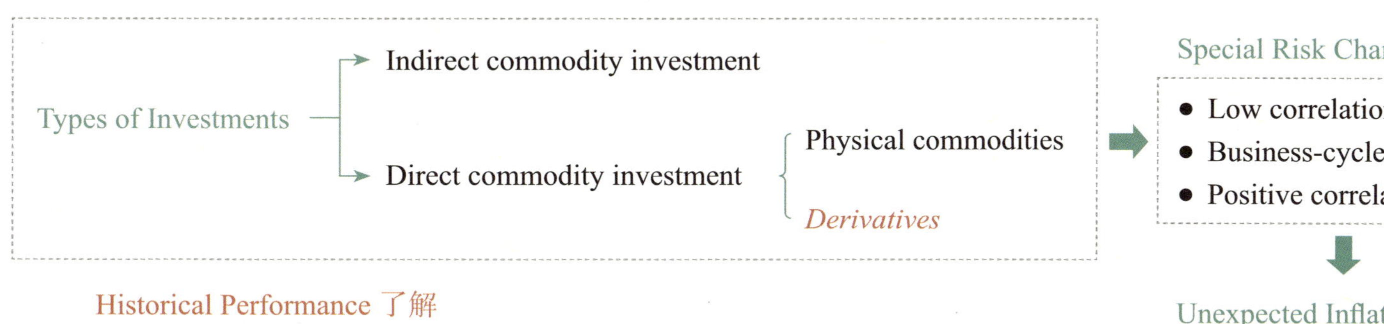

Historical Performance 了解

Special Risk Characteristics

- Low correlation with stocks and bonds
- Business-cycle sensitivity
- Positive correlation with inflation

抗非预期通胀前提

Unexpected Inflation Hedge ★

- *Storable commodities*
- *Intensity of economic activity*

Hedge Funds

分类★

- *Equity market neutral* → Beta = 0，保留大量非系统性风险
- *Convertible arbitrage strategies* → long bond，short stock
- *Fixed-income arbitrage* → long and short positions in fixed income
- *Distressed securities investments* → long bond of bankruptcy company
- *Merger arbitrage or deal arbitrage* → long target stock，short acquirer
- *Hedged equity strategies* → equity long-short
- *Global macro strategies* → top down，与 managed futures 相似
- *Emerging markets funds*
- *FOF*

Compensation Structure ★

- AUM fee of about 1% ～ 2%
- Incentive fees of 20%
- High-water marks
- Lock-up period limit

Fund of Funds ★

- Diversification
- Extra layer of fees
- More liquidity
- Cash drag (keeping extra cash)
- Good entry-level investment
- Less survivorship bias and backfill bias
- Better indicator
- Suffer from style drift
- More highly correlation with equity markets

Benchmark Bias ★

- Popularity bias
- Survivorship bias
- Stale price
- Backfill or inclusion bias

Performance Evaluation Concerns ★★

Historical Performance 了解

The Returns Achieved

- Calculated monthly
- Compounded annualized
- Leverage：Fully paid assumption

复利周期影响 return

- ➢ Funds allow *entry or exit* to their funds quarterly
- ➢ *No compounding* is typically applied to the loss

Rolling return (RR)：*Consistent of returns*，*identify cyclicality*

Volatility and Downside Volatility

- *Standard deviation* is a *common measure*
- *Calculated* based on *monthly returns (square root of 12)*
- *Normal distribution* → *Incorrect (high kurtosis* and *negative skewness)*

Semideviation 替代方法

$$\textit{Downside Deviation} = \sqrt{\frac{\sum_{i=1}^{n}\left[\min\left(r_t - r^*,\ 0\right)\right]^2}{n-1}}$$

Another popular risk measure is *drawdown*

Sharpe Ratio has Limitations

- Time dependent，asymmetrical return distribution
- Illiquid bias the SR upward，can be gamed
- Serially correlated return overestimate SR
- Ignor correlations with other assets in a portfolio

Performance Appraisal Measures

- Sortino ratio
- Gain-to-loss ratio

Correlations

- Provide information on diversification
- Meaningful when normally distributed
- Need to consider skewness and kurtosis for HF

Skewness and Kurtosis

- Skewness → measure asymmetry
- Kurtosis → evaluates the incidence of returns clustered near versus far away from the mean

Managed Futures

Managed Futures vs. Hedge Funds

- Limited partnership
- Same compensational scheme for managers (base fees plus performance fees，e.g. 2-plus-20)
- Skill-based investment strategies
- Absolute return strategies
- More than one way to categorize subgroups
- 与 Global Macro 最相似

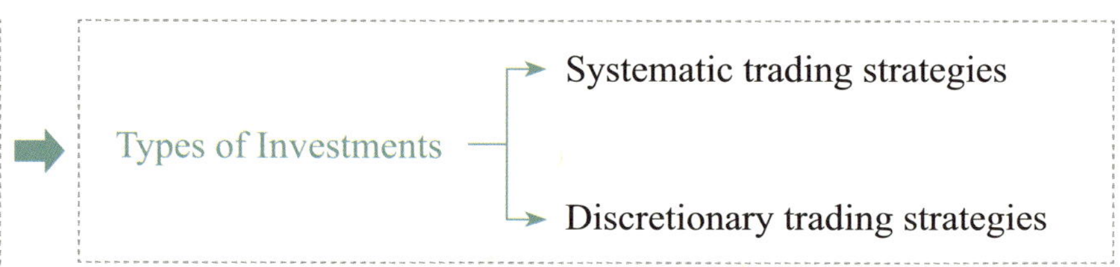

Investment Characteristics

- "Zero-sum" games
- Hedgers may pay a risk premium to liquidity providers for insurance they obtain
- Hedgers earn less than the risk-free rate
- CTAs attempt to conduct arbitrage
- Actively follow momentum strategies
- Short positions can earn positive excess returns in falling markets
- Option markets exploit changes in market volatility (one of the determinants of option value)

Historical Performance 了解

Distressed Securities

Types of Assets Distressed Securities

- The publicly traded debt and equity
- Fallen Angels
- Orphan equity
- Bank debt and trade claims
- "Lender of last resort" notes
- A variety of derivative instruments

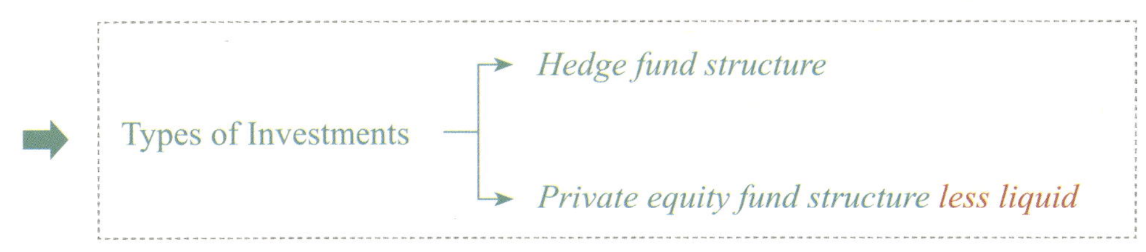

Strategies of Distressed Securities Investing

Hedge fund

Long-only value investing

- Hope will rise in value
- High-yield investing
- Orphan equity investing

Distressed debt arbitrage

- Purchasing a company's distressed debt and selling the company's equity short
- Popular with hedge funds

PE

Vulture funds

- Becomes major creditor to influence BOD
- Assists in the recovery or reorganization process

A variation of active approach

- Convert distressed debt to private equity
- Becomes owner on favorable terms
- Sell the company after restoring the company to better health

Risks

- Event risk
- Liquidity risk
- Market risk
- J factor risk

Historical Performance 了解

第 10 章

Risk Management

Reading 27

RISK MANAGEMENT

ERM System

ERM System

Risk Management Governance

概念，本章框架

- ✓ **Identify** each risk factor
- ✓ **Quantify** the factor in measurable terms
  - Risk in a single aggregate measure
  - Risk contributes to the overall risk of the firm
- ✓ Setting **capital requirements**

Governance	Description	Characteristics
Centralized	Single risk management group controls risk	• Permit economies of scale • Enterprise-level risk estimates may be lower than those derived from individual units • Put the responsibility on a level closer to senior management, which is deemed reasonable
Decentralized	Individual business unit manage risk	Allowing people closer to the actual risk taking to more directly manage it

Identify Risk ★

Identify Risk

Risk Types	Definition
Market risk ★	Related to changes in interest rates, exchange rates, equity prices, commodity prices, and so on
Credit risk ★	Defined here as the risk of loss caused by a counterparty's or debtor's failure to make a promised payment
Liquidity risk ★	The possibility of sustaining significant losses due to the inability to take or liquidate a position quickly at a fair price
Operations risk ★	The potential for failures in the firm's operating systems, including its ERM system, due to personal, technological, mechanical, or other problems
Settlement risk	One party could be making a payment while the other side of the exchange could be in the process of defaulting and fail to deliver on the transaction
Model risk	Models are only as good as their construction and inputs
Sovereign risk	The willingness and ability of a foreign government to repay its obligations
Regulatory risk	Different securities in the portfolio can fall under different regulatory bodies
Other risks	Include political risk, tax risk, accounting risk, and legal risk, which relate directly or indirectly to changes in the political climate

Measuring Risks

衡量 Market Risk

- Standard deviation
- First-order projection → β，δ，D
- Second order techniques → *Gamma*，*C*
- VAR ★★ 概念，计算

The 1-day，1% VAR of a portfolio is \$2.6M（会写）
- There is a 1% chance the portfolio will lose at least \$2.6M in one day
- We are 99% confident that the portfolio will lose no more than \$2.6M in one day

$$VAR\ (X\%) = z_{X\%} \times \sigma$$

$$VAR_{dollar} = VAR\ (X\%) \times asset\ value = z_{X\%} \times \sigma \times asset\ value$$

考点
- VAR 有 % 与 \$ 的形式
- VAR 不同期限转换 → 平方根法则
- VAR 不同置信区间转换 → 95% 对应 1.65 标准差，99% 对应 2.33 标准差

三种计算方法
- Analytical method (variance-covariance/delta normal method)
- Historical method
- Monte Carlo method → 计算同 analytical method

VAR 计算方法的优缺点比较★★

Analytical Method

Advantages

- Easy to calculate and understand
- Model the correlations of risks
- Can be applied to different time periods according to industry custom

Disadvantages

- Assume a normal distribution
- Many assets exhibit leptokurtosis
- Difficulty in estimating correlations in very large portfolios

Historical Method

Advantages

- Nonparametric
- Applied to different time periods

Disadvantage

- Relies completely on events of the past, and distribution prevailed in the past might not hold in the future

Monte Carlo Method

Advantages

- No need of normal distribution

Disadvantages

- Require a sufficiently large number of simulations to get the true population VAR
- GIGO
- The complex method can lead to false sense of overconfidence
- Costly to implement the simulation

VAR 本身的优缺点

✓ *Advantages*

- It has become the industry standard for risk measurement and is required by many regulators
- It aggregates all risk into one single, easy to understand number
- It can be used in capital allocation

✓ *Limitations*

- Some of the methods (Monte Carlo) are difficult and expensive
- The different computation methods can generate different estimates of VAR
- It can generate a false sense of security
- It is one-sided, focusing on the left tail in the return distribution, and ignores any upside potential

与 VAR 配合使用的风险评估工具

- Back-tested
- Incremental VAR (IVAR)
- Cash flow at risk (CFAR)
- Earnings at risk (EAR)
- Tail value at risk (TVAR) ★概念
- Credit VAR
- Stress testing ★方法，优缺点

概念

Scenario Analysis

Stylized Scenarios	It involves simulating a movement in at least one interest rate, exchange rate, stock price, or commodity price relevant to the portfolio
Actual Extreme Events	Focuses on the events that have occurred in the past but may have a higher probability than given by the probability model or specific historic time period used in the VAR estimate
Hypothetical Events	Focuses on the events that have not occurred and are assigned a low probability

Stress Testing

Factor Push Analysis	Push a factor or factors to the extreme
Maximum Loss Optimization	Identify risk factors that have the greatest potential impacts
Worst-case Scenario	Simultaneously push all factors to the extreme

衡量 Credit Risk

- Current credit risk
- Potential credit risk 计算，就是衍生品求 value ★

Contract	Credit Risk
Forward	*No current credit risk* until expiration *Potential credit risk = Value = PV inflows − PV outflows*
Swaps	Interest rate swap： Highest risk around the *middle*
	Currency swap： Highest risk between the *middle* and *maturity* of the agreement
Options	Only born by the *long position*
	✓ European option ● *No current credit risk* until expiration ● *Potential credit risk = Value estimated by valuation model* (e.g. BSM model) or *option premium* (if no value is given)
	✓ *American option* credit risk is *at least as great as* European option ✓ *Only* American option *has current credit risk* before expiration ● *Current credit risk = Intrinsic Value* ● *Potential credit risk = Value estimated by valuation model* (e.g. BSM model) or *option premium* (if no value is given)

Managing Risks

Managing Market Risk

- Risk budgeting → VAR
- Performance stopouts
- Working capital allocations
- VAR limits
- Scenario analysis
- Risk factor limits
- Position concentration limits
- Leverage limits
- Liquidity limits

Managing Credit Risk

- Limit exposure to any individual debtor
- Marking to market
- Collateral
- Payment netting
- Closeout netting
- Minimum credit standards
- Transfer risk to others；CDS

Measure Risk-adjusted Performance

计算，比较业绩好坏

$$Treynor\ R = \frac{R_P - R_F}{\beta} \quad SharpeR = \frac{R_P - R_F}{\sigma} \quad SortinoR = \frac{\bar{R}_P - MAR}{\sigma_{downside}}$$

$$RoMAD = \frac{\bar{R}_P}{max.drawdown} \quad InformationR_P = \frac{active\ return}{active\ risk} = \frac{R_P - R_B}{\sigma_{(R_P - R_B)}}$$

→

Capital Allocation

- Nominal，notional，or monetary position limits
- VAR-based position limits
- Maximum loss limits
- Internal capital requirements
- Regulatory capital requirements

优缺点

第 11 章

Risk Management Applications of Derivatives

Reading 28

RISK MANAGEMENT APPLICATIONS OF FORWARD AND FUTURES STRATEGIES

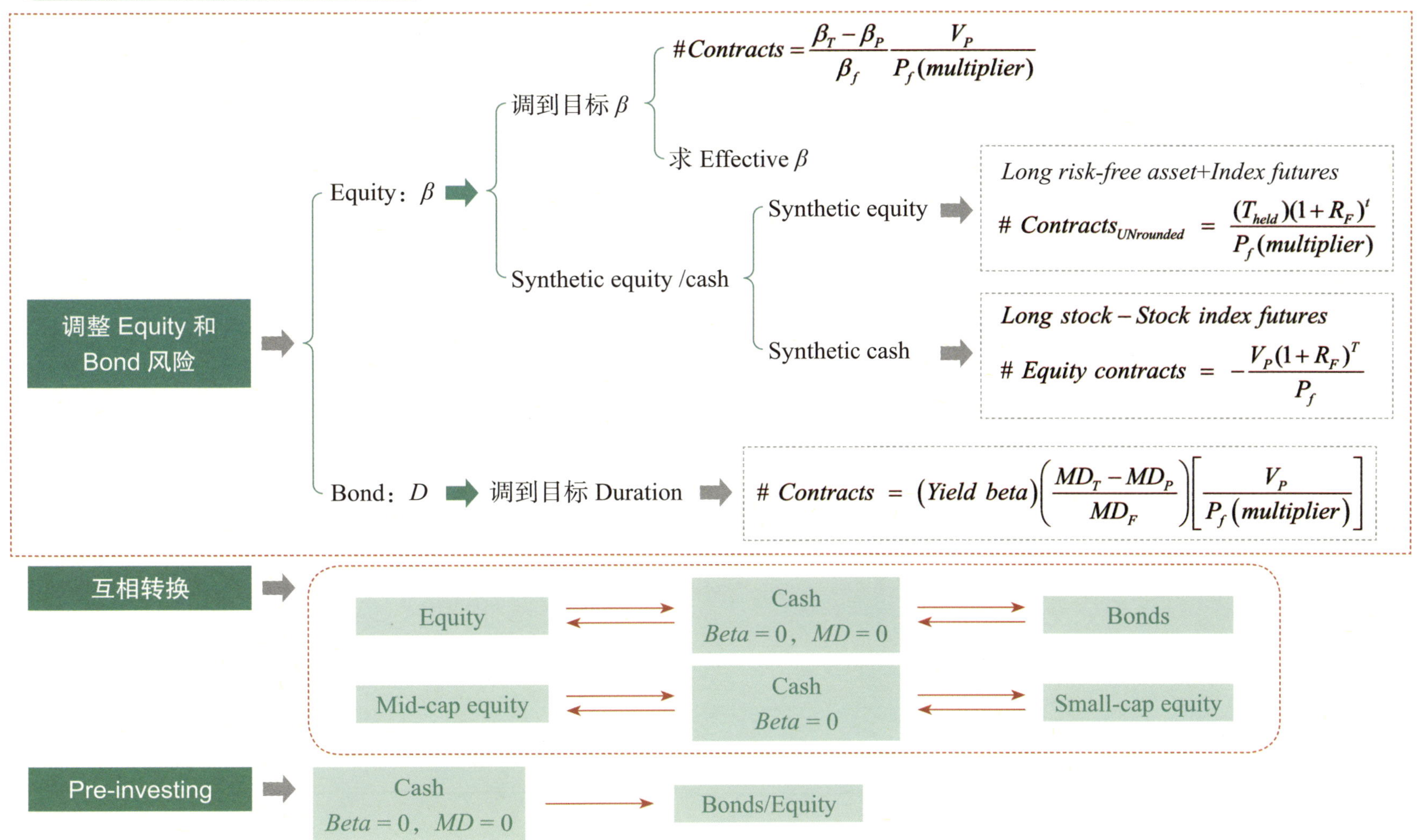

Domestic ★★
都是常规计算，多做例题即可
调整 Equity 和 Bond 风险
Equity：β
调到目标 β
$\#Contracts = \frac{\beta_T - \beta_P}{\beta_f}\frac{V_P}{P_f(multiplier)}$
求 Effective β
Synthetic equity /cash
Synthetic equity
Long risk-free asset+Index futures
$\#\ Contracts_{UNrounded} = \frac{(T_{held})(1+R_F)^t}{P_f(multiplier)}$
Synthetic cash
Long stock – Stock index futures
$\#\ Equity\ contracts = -\frac{V_P(1+R_F)^T}{P_f}$
Bond：D
调到目标 Duration
$\#\ Contracts = (Yield\ beta)\left(\frac{MD_T - MD_P}{MD_F}\right)\left[\frac{V_P}{P_f(multiplier)}\right]$
互相转换
Equity
Cash
$Beta = 0$，$MD = 0$
Bonds
Mid-cap equity
Cash
$Beta = 0$
Small-cap equity
Pre-investing
Cash
$Beta = 0$，$MD = 0$
Bonds/Equity

Foreign Currency Risk 了解

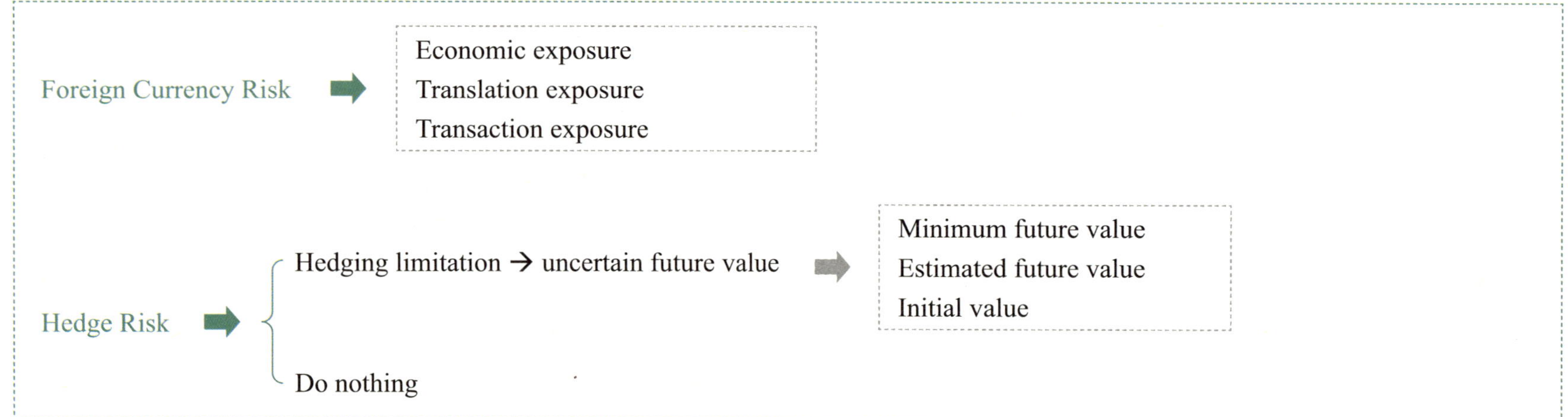

Reading 29

RISK MANAGEMENT APPLICATIONS OF OPTION STRATEGIES

Option Strategies for Equity Portfolios ★★

考法 → 构成
Max Profit & Loss
Breakeven point

Covered Call & Protective Put

- Covered call = Short call + long stock → Profit = $(S_T - S_0) - [\max\{0, (S_T - X)\} - C]$
- Protective Put = Long stock + long put → Profit = $(S_T - S_0) + [\max\{0, (X - S_T)\} - P]$

Money Spread

一个 strategy 只用 call 或者 put，而不是二者混用

Bull spread	Call	Bull Call Spread = Long call at X_L + short call at X_H → Profit = $[\max\{0, (S_T - X_L)\} - C_L] - [\max\{0, (S_T - X_H)\} - C_H]$
	Put	Bull Put Spread = Long put at X_L + short put at X_H → Profit = $[\max\{0, (X_L - S_T)\} - P_L] - [\max\{0, (X_H - S_T)\} - P_H]$
Bear spread	Call	Bear Call Spread = Short call at X_L + long call at X_H → Profit = $-[\max\{0, (S_T - X_L)\} - C_L] + [\max\{0, (S_T - X_H)\} - C_H]$
	Put	Bear Put Spread = Short put at X_L + long put at X_H → Profit = $-[\max\{0, (X_L - S_T)\} - P_L] + [\max\{0, (X_H - S_T)\} - P_H]$
Butterfly spread	Call	Butterfly Spread Using Calls = Long call at X_L + long call at X_H + short two calls at X_M → Profit = $[\max\{0, (S_T - X_L)\} - C_L] + [\max\{0, (S_T - X_H)\} - C_H] - 2[\max\{0, (S_T - X_M)\} - C_M]$
	Put	Butterfly Spread Using Puts = Long put at X_L + long put at X_H + short two puts at X_M → Profit = $[\max\{0, (X_L - S_T)\} - P_L] + [\max\{0, (X_H - S_T)\} - P_H] - 2[\max\{0, (X_M - S_T)\} - P_M]$

Combinations of Calls and Puts

Straddle	*Long straddle = Long call + long put* ● This strategy is profitable when the stock price *moves strongly in either direction*. This strategy *bets on volatility*
	Short straddle = Short call + short put ● Bets on *little movement in the stock*
Collar	*Collar = protective put + covered call = Long stock + short call + long put* ● If the premium of the two are equal， it is called a *zero-cost collar*
Box spread	*Box Spread = Bull call spread + bear put spread* ● If the options are priced correctly， the payoff must be the *risk-free*

Interest Rate Option ★

都是常规计算，多做例题即可

Call/Put	Call：Floating-rate *borrower* Put：Floating-rate *investor*
	计算 Effective annual rate
Cap/Floor/Collar	计算 period payment

Option Portfolio Risk Management Strategies ★★

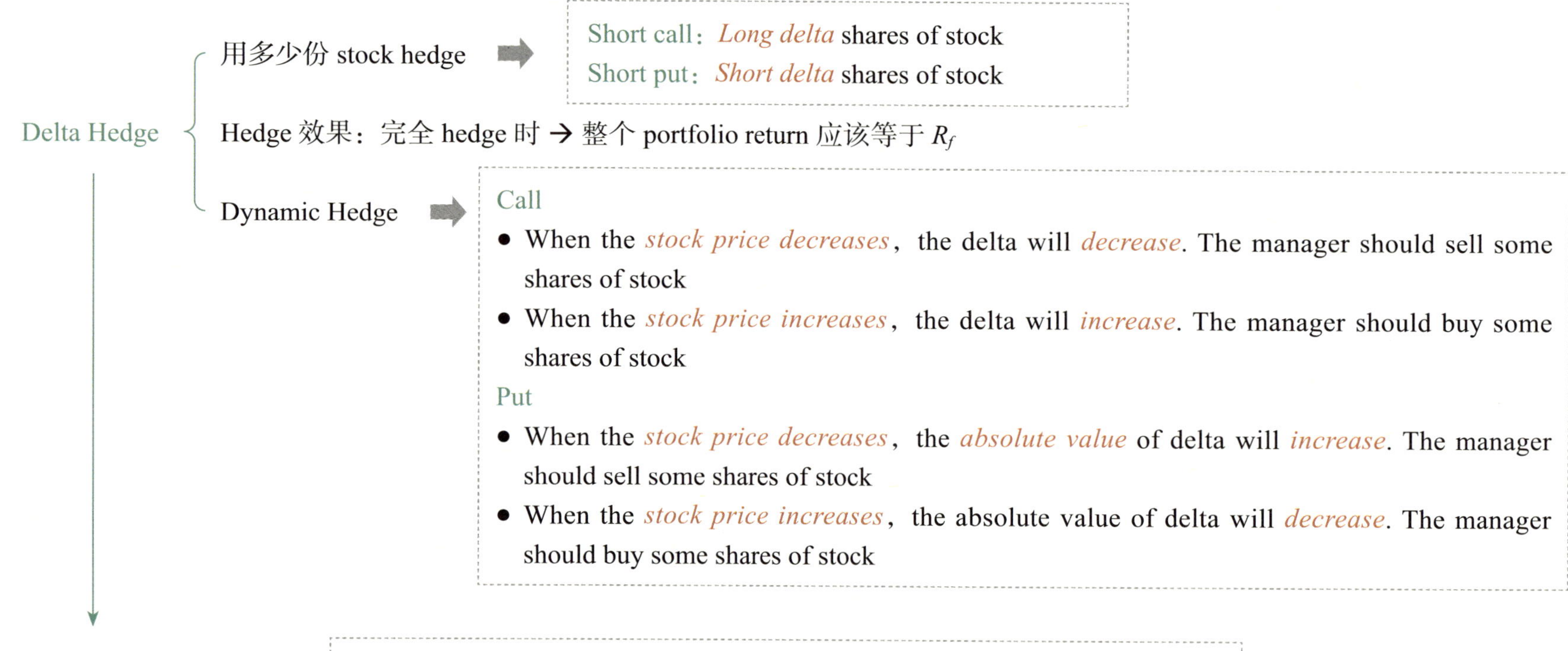

Reading 30

RISK MANAGEMENT APPLICATIONS OF SWAP STRATEGIES

Interest Rate Swap ★★

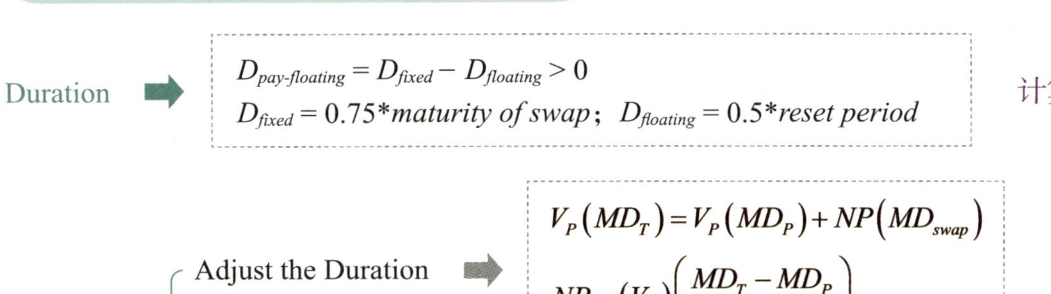

Duration →

$D_{pay\text{-}floating} = D_{fixed} - D_{floating} > 0$

$D_{fixed} = 0.75*maturity\ of\ swap$；$D_{floating} = 0.5*reset\ period$

计算

应用 →

- Adjust the Duration →

  $$V_P(MD_T) = V_P(MD_P) + NP(MD_{swap})$$

  $$NP = (V_P)\left(\frac{MD_T - MD_P}{MD_{swap}}\right)$$

- Convert between Floating-Rate Loan and Fixed-Rate Loan →

  Market Value Risk and Cash Flow Risk
  - Cash flow risk：A concern with floating-rate instruments
  - Market value risk：A concern with fixed-rate instruments

  改变公司 Floating-rate Liability
  - Enters a *pay-fixed*，*receive-floating swap* to change the nature of a floating-rate liability

- Manage the Risk of Structured Notes
  - Leveraged Floating-Rate Notes
  - Inverse Floaters

Currency Swap ★★

都是常规计算，多做例题即可

应用

1. Convert a Loan in One Currency into Another

Cash flows for a plain vanilla currency swap

Swap dealer

6% on €10 M

LIBOR on $15 M

6.1% on €10 M

US Company

German Company

6% on €10 M

LIBOR on $15 M

€10 million bonds at 6%

$15 million FRN at LIBOR

2. Currency Swap for Lower Cost

3. Currency Swap without Changes of NP

Equity Swap ★

Equity 与 Bond 头寸转换　应用

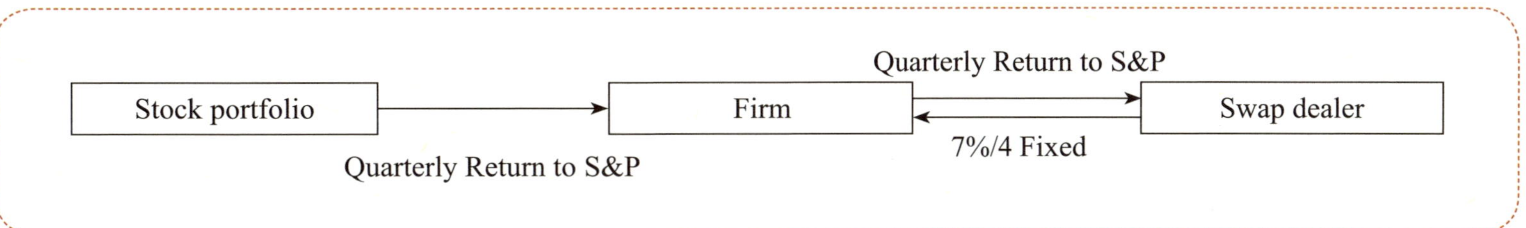

Interest Rate Swaptions ★★

Payer swaption	Gives the buyer the right to be the fixed rate payer If *market interest rates are high*， the swaption will be *exercised*
	= interest rate call option
Receiver swaption	Gives the buyer the right to be the fixed-rate receiver If *market interest rates are low*， the swaption will be *exercised*
	= interest rate put option

应用 

1. Using Swaption to Convert Loans 
   - The payer swaption would convert a future floating-rate loan to a fixed-rate loan
   - The receiver swaption would convert a future fixed-rate loan to a floating-rate loan
2. Using Swaption to Terminate a Swap
3. Synthetically Adding or Removing a Call Feature
   - Adding a Call Feature → long receiver swaption
   - Removing a Call Feature → short receiver swaption

第 12 章

Trading，Monitoring and Rebalancing

Reading 31

EXECUTION OF PORTFOLIO DECISIONS

Source of Trading Cost

交易成本的来源

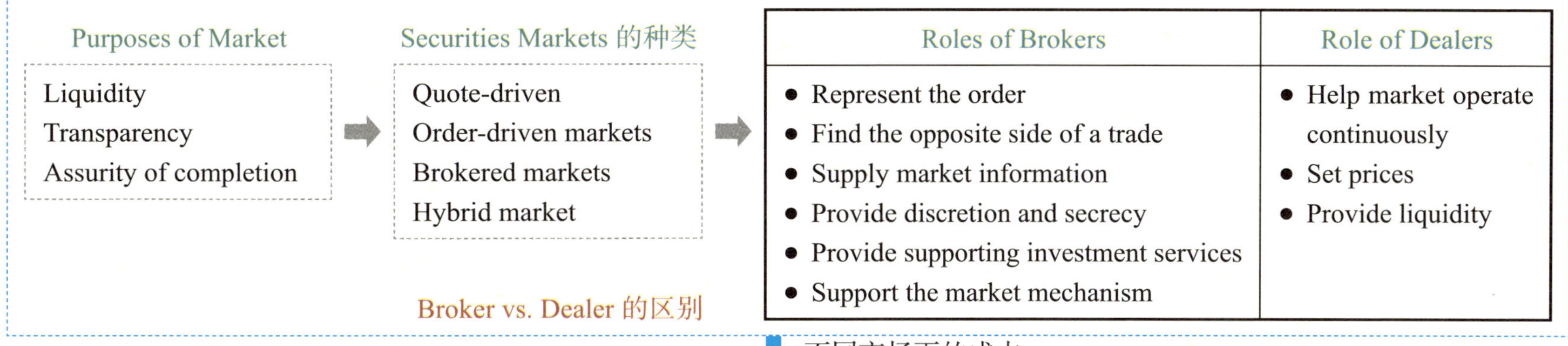

不同市场下的成本

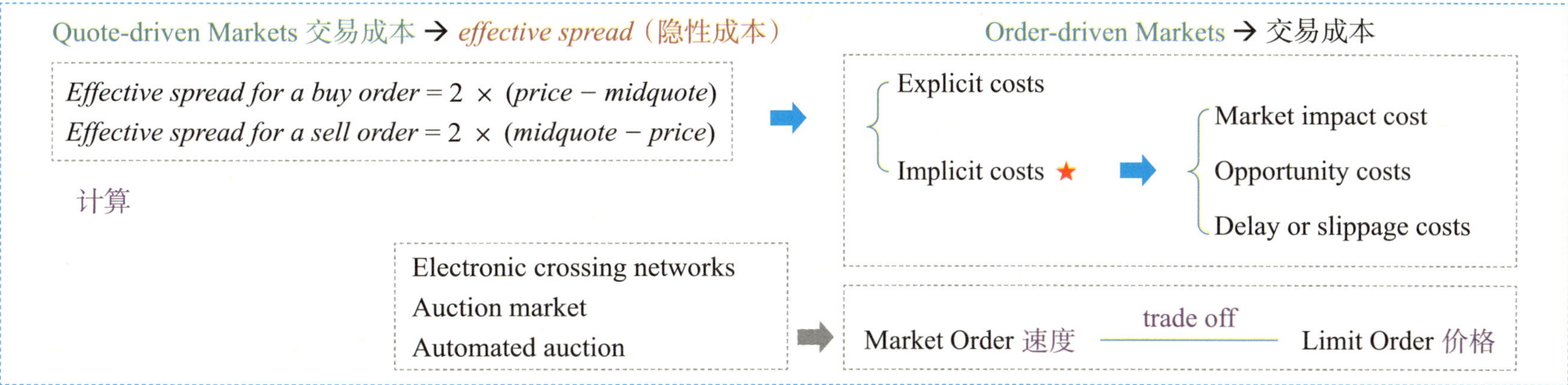

Measurement of Trading Cost

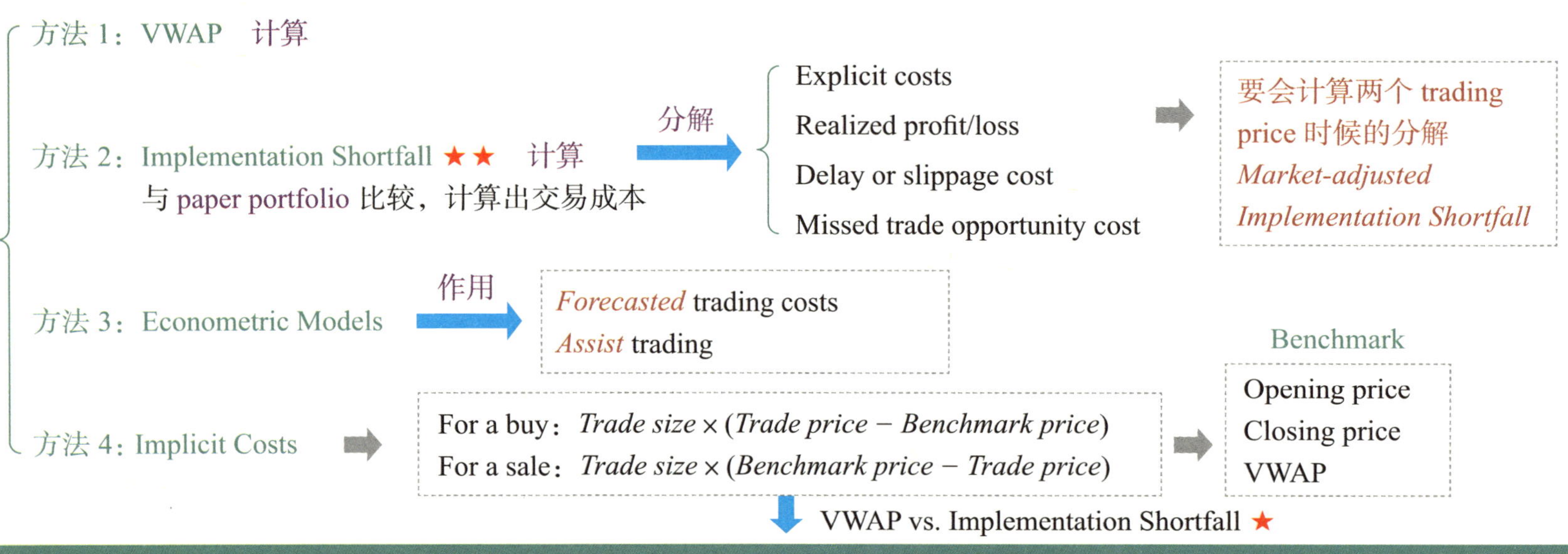

	Advantage	Disadvantage
VWAP	• Easily understood • Computationally simple • Can be applied • Appropriate for small trades	• Trades that dominate trading volume • Can be gamed by traders • Does not evaluate delayed orders • Fail to account market movement/trade volume
Implementation Shortfall	• Shows cost of implementing managers' ideas • Show tradeoff → quick execution and market impact • Decomposes and identifies costs • Optimizer to minimize trading costs • Not subject to gaming	• May be unfamiliar to traders • Requires considerable data and analysis

Practical Issues

Major Trader Types

Trader	Motivation	Trading Time Horizon	Time versus Price Preference
Information-motivated	New information	Minutes to hours	Time
Value-motivated	Perceived valuation errors	Days to weeks	Price
Liquidity-motivated	Invest cash or divest securities	Minutes to hours	Time
Passive	Rebalancing，investing/divesting cash	Days to weeks	Price
Dealers and day traders	Accommodation	Minutes to hours	Passive，indifferent

不依托 Trader 主观判断

Algorithmic Trading ★

概念，区分不同的适用范围

Reading 32

MONITORING AND REBALANCING

Monitoring and Rebalancing

Monitoring

更新个人 IPS，会在 IPS 中考

Rebalancing

Benefit of Rebalancing

- Maintaining desired risk exposure
- Rebalancing also provides discipline

Costs of Rebalancing

- Transactions costs and tax liability
- Market impact for institutional investor

Optimal Corridor Width ★★

- Transaction costs (+)
- Risk tolerance (+)
- Correlation with rest of portfolio (+)
- Asset class volatility (−)
- Volatility of rest of portfolio (−)

Rebalancing Disciplines　控制成本 vs. 调整频率

Calendar Rebalancing

- Predetermined，regular basis
- Benefit：Provides discipline
- Drawback：Could differ significantly from its optimal weights

Percentage-of-Portfolio

- Referred to percent range rebalancing or interval rebalancing
- $Corridor = T \pm (P \times T)$

Calendar-and-percentage-of Portfolio Rebalancing

- Mitigates the problem of rebalancing *near the optimum*

Equal Probability Rebalancing

Tactical Rebalancing

Rebalancing to Target Weight vs. to Allowed Range → halfway back

Dynamic Rebalancing Strategies ★ ★

掌握 rebalance 方法

Buy and Hold

- 不做调整
- 有 floor value
- Linear → $M = 1$

Constant-Mix

- Stock price 上升 → sell，下降 → buy
- 无 floor value
- 波动市场表现最好
- Concave → $M < 1$

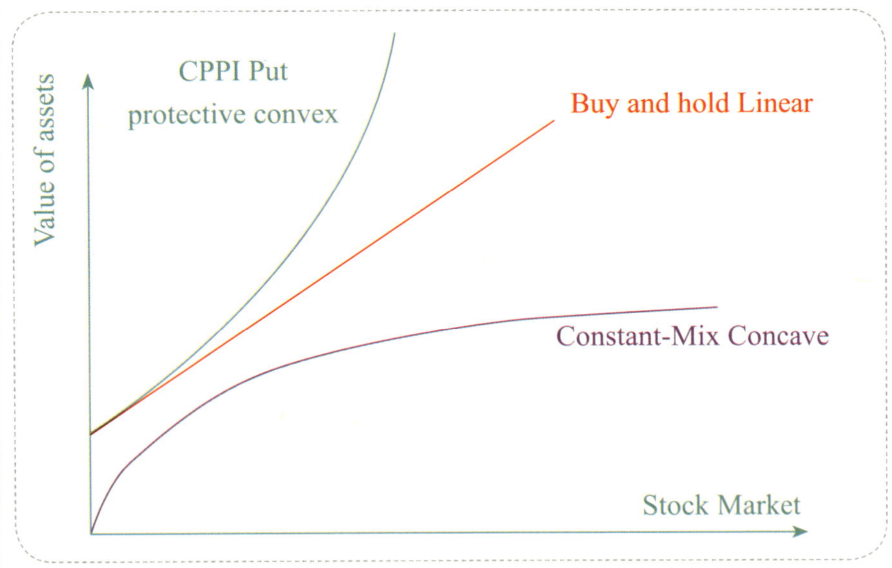

CPPI

- Stock price 上升 → buy，下降 → sell
- 有 Floor value → cushion
- Trending 市场表现最好
- *Target equities investment* = *M* (*portfolio value* − *floor value*)
- Convex → $M > 1$

第 13 章

Performance Evaluation

Reading 33

EVALUATING PORTFOLIO PERFORMANCE

Evaluating Portfolio Performance

Evaluating Portfolio Performance

- The Fund Sponsor's Perspective → 外部评估
- The Investment Manager's Perspective → 内部评估

1. Performance Measurement

计算★★

↓ 三步

TWRR→ 剔除 External cash flows

$$r_t = \frac{MV_1 - (MV_0 + CF)}{MV_0 + CF}$$

发生在期初

$$r_t = \frac{(MV_1 - CF) - MV_0}{MV_0}$$

发生在期末

→

TWRR

发生在期间 → 分段计算并用几何平均汇总

→

Data quality

- *Illiquid* (infrequently priced) assets
- *Thinly traded fixed-income securities*
- Should include *trade date accounting*

MWRR→ 求 *IRR*，会按计算器，注意计算结果为 1 天的 *IRR*

MWRR

- An average growth rate of all funds
- It is affected external cash flows
- 适用于 manager 对外部 *CF* 有控制
- 只在期初、期末求 *MV*

TWRR

- Not affected by external cash flows
- 适用于 manager 对外部 *CF* 无控制（常见）
- 有 *CF* 时求 *MV*
- 资产流动性差时数据获得有问题

 结合

LIRR

2. Performance Attribution

原理 → $P = M + S + A$ 将 R_p 切分，得到 return 来源，计算 M，S，A

⬇ 首先，找到 Benchmark

Benchmark 相关

Benchmark properties (SAMURAI)

- Specified in advance
- Appropriate
- Measurable
- Unambiguous
- Reflective of the manager's current investment opinions
- Accountable
- Investable

7 种常见 Benchmark

- Absolute
- Manager universes ★
- Broad market indices
- Style indices
- Factor-model-based
- Returns-based
- Custom security-based

优缺点★

检查 Benchmark 的好坏

- Minimum systematic bias
- Minimum tracking error
- Similar risk characteristics
- A high coverage ratio
- Turnover
- Positive active position

★根据条件判断 Benchmark 的好坏

⬇ 根据 Benchmark 做业绩归因

- *Macro Attribution*
- *Micro Attribution*
  - Allocation/Selection Attribution — *Stock*
  - Fundamental Factor Model — *Stock*
  - Fixed-income Portfolio Return Attribution — *Bond*

业绩归因 ★★

Macro performance attribution → fund sponsor level

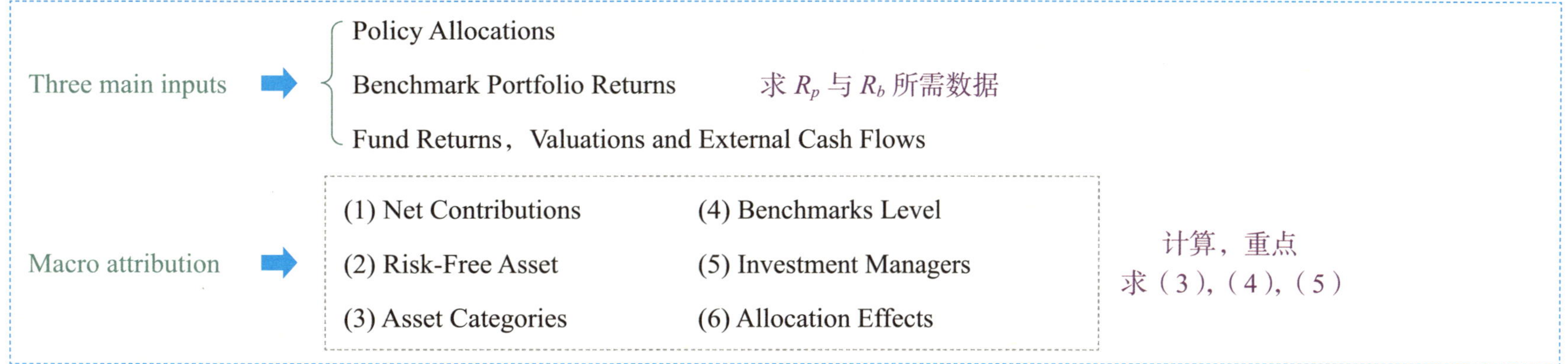

Micro performance attribution → manager level 计算

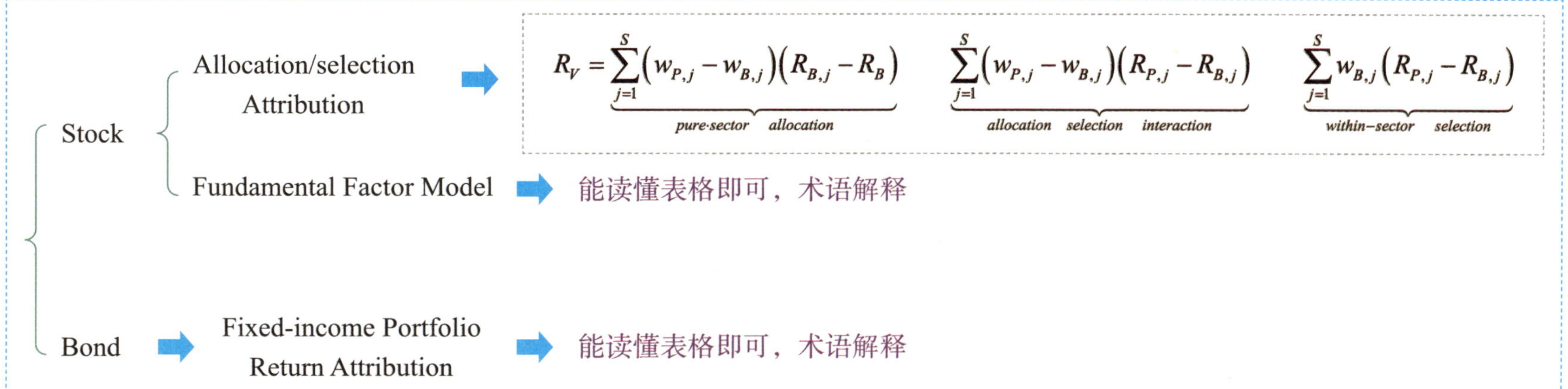

Risk Adjusted Return

3. Performance Appraisal

Ex-Post Alpha

$\alpha_A = R_{At} - E(R_A)$

Treynor Measure

$$T_A = \frac{\bar{R}_A - \bar{R}_F}{\beta_A}$$

Systematic risk

Sharpe Ratio

$$S_A = \frac{\bar{R}_A - \bar{R}_F}{\sigma_A}$$

M2 Measure（同 SR）

$$M_P^2 = \bar{R}_F + \left(\frac{\bar{R}_P - \bar{R}_F}{\sigma_P}\right)\sigma_M$$

Total risk

The Information Ratio

$$IR_A = \frac{\bar{R}_A - \bar{R}_B}{\sigma_{A-B}}$$

Relative risk

 根据业绩表现判断 manager 是否留用

假设检验★

- ✓ **H_0**：The manager adds no value
- ✓ **H_1**：The manager adds positive value
  - Type I error：Keeping managers with zero value-added
  - Type II error：Firing managers with positive value-added

Quality Control Charts

Manager Continuation Policy (MCP)

- ✓ One performance period is insufficient
- ✓ Develop formal policies
- ✓ Use other information in evaluating
  - Strategy applied consistently
  - Relevant benchmark used
  - Personnel turnover
  - Growth in the account

第 14 章

Global Investment Performance Standards (GIPS)

使用说明

- 从 2007 年开始，GIPS 就没有出过上午题，都是以下午题的形式来考察的，那么把重要条款看熟即可，不需要严格背诵
- 有些年份可能没有考到 GIPS，但在一般情况下，下午题都会有一个 case 出到，占比也不大，为了达到事半功倍的效果，复习时着重看重要条款
- 本资料根据历年 mock 和原版书课后题，只列出重要条款，而且是根据试题当中的题目形式做的整理，希望可以帮助大家快速理清条款内容。建议大家在考前多翻两遍

——李斯克 & 何旋

GIPS 出题形式：
问题一：给定 composite performance presentation 的表格，表格当中必须要有的数据
问题二：在说明段 (notes) 当中，哪些是必须要 disclosure 的？题干当中漏掉了必须要 disclosure 的哪一项？
→ 对应条款：*4. Disclosure & 5. Presentation and Reporting*（需要大家重点记忆的条款）
问题三：其他关于原理性的问题，需要掌握的条款

GIPS 结构

0 ～ 5：关于 general portfolio 的要求（stock & bond portfolio）★★
6：Real estate（了解）
7：PE（了解）
8：Wrap fee/SMA portfolio（主要是 pension fund，了解）

表格当中必须要有的数据

或有关系，两者只要有一个就可以

Sample 1
Investment Firm
Balanced Growth Composite
1 January 2002 through 31 December 2001

也可以是 composite assets as a percentage of total firm assets

Year	Composite Cross Return (%)	Composite Net Return (%)	Custom Benchmark Return (%)	Composite 3-Yr St Dev (%)	Benchmark 3-Yr St Dev (%)	Number of Portfolios	Internal Dispersion (%)	Composite Assets ($ M)	Firm Assets ($ M)
2002	−10.5	−11.4	−11.8			31	4.5	165	236
2003	16.3	15.1	13.2			34	2.0	235	346
2004	7.5	6.4	8.9			38	5.7	344	529
2005	1.8	0.8	0.3			45	2.8	445	695
2006	11.2	10.1	12.2			48	3.1	520	839
2007	6.1	5.0	7.1			49	2.8	505	1 014
2008	−21.3	−22.1	−24.9			44	2.9	475	964
2009	16.5	15.3	14.7			47	3.1	493	983
2010	10.6	9.5	13.0			51	3.5	549	1 114
2011	2.7	1.7	0.4	7.1	7.4	54	2.5	575	1 236

另外一种形式

Sample 2
Asset Management Company
Active World Equity Composite
Creation Date：1 July 2005
Reporting Currency：EUR

Year	Cross Return (%)	XYZ World Index Return (%)	Dispersion (Range) (%)	# of Portfolios	Composite Assets (€ M))	% of Firm Assets
2011	−1.9	−0.5	0.2	6	224.9	2.1
2010	16.3	13.5	0.7	8	256.7	2.0
2009	29.0	25.8	1.5	8	205.6	1.9
2008	−39.8	−36.4	1.3	7	164.1	1.5
2007	−2.8	−2.7	n/a	≤ 5	143.7	1.2
2006	9.3	7.5	n/a	≤ 5	62.8	0.4
2005①	14.2	12.6	n/a	≤ 5	16.1	< 0.1

Year	Composite 3-Yr St Dev (%)	Benchmark 3-Yr St Dev (%)
2011	12.9	14.6
2010	13.2	14.1
2009	17.0	16.3
2008	15.6	14.2

① Returns are for the period from 1 July 2005 (inception date) through 31 December 2005.

注意

1. The number of portfolios in the composite as of each annual period end. If *the composite contains ≤ 5 portfolios* at period end，the number of portfolios is not required
2. Returns for periods of *less than one year must not be annualized*
3. If a composite includes non-fee-paying portfolios，the firm must present the *percentage of composite assets represented by non-fee-paying portfolios as of each annual period end*

Disclosure (Notes)：Required

1. Claim：标准的说明段

[Insert name of FIRM] claims compliance with the Global Investment Performance Standards (GIPS®) and has prepared and presented this report in compliance with the GIPS standards

注意：Verification

（1）Verification 是自愿的，如果被 verification → [Insert name of FIRM] has been independently verified for the periods [insert dates]. *The verification report(s) is/are available upon request*

（2）如果没有被 verification，可以不用讲上面那段话

（3）A single verification report is issued with respect to the *whole firm*. Verification cannot be carried out on a composite

（4）Verification must be performed by a qualified *independent third party*

2. Firm：定义段 (organizationally and functionally segregated)

例如：Sample 1 Investment Firm is a balanced portfolio investment manager that invests solely in US-based securities. Sample 1 Investment Firm is defined as an independent investment management firm that is not affiliated with any parent organization（摘自 Sample 1）

3. Composite：Return，定义，日期，货币，风险（内在与自身）→ 必须要有的

（1）Gross of fee return or net of fee return（两者有一个就可以）

- 要 disclose gross of fee return 和 net of fee return 都是扣了什么费用
- Gross of fee return 是扣了 trading expense
- Net of fee return 是在 gross of fee return 的基础上又扣了 management fee，还有可能有 performance fee
- Custody fee 不属于 trading expense。所以 gross of fee return 里不扣 custody fee，net of fee return 里才扣

（2）Composite description

（3）Create date

（4）Currency

（5）Internal dispersion（有 5 种方法可以算，了解算法，但是必须要有说明段说明是用哪种方法）

- Highest and lowest returns earned by portfolios that were in the composite for the full year
- Or alternatively，High/Low range
- The equal-weighted stand deviation of returns to portfolios in the composite
- The asset-weighted stand deviation
- The interquartile range—the difference between the returns in the first and third quartiles of the distribution

（6）Three-year annualized ex-post standard deviation 计算方法的说明段（using monthly return，所以是 36 个数据求标准差，怎么求的大家不用掌握，但是对标准差的求法要有说明段）

（7）Fee schedule 说明段

4. Benchmark → 必须要有的

（1）Benchmark description
（2）Return
（3）Three-year annualized ex-post standard deviation

5. Portfolio → 必须要有"计算 portfolio 收益的 policies 是 available upon request"

6. 总结：三个客户有需要可以获得的标准段

✧ 必须要有的：

- List of composite description
- Policy and procedures of calculation，valuation，preparing COMPLIANT PRESENTATIONS are available upon request

✧ 如果公司被 verification：

- Verification report(s) is/are available upon request（但是如果公司没有被 verification，这个可以不说）

Disclosure (Notes)：或有披露

1. Minimum asset level
   - ✧ 如果 composite 有 minimum asset level，则需要披露，但是一个 composite 不一定要有 minimum asset level
   - ✧ 如果有 minimum asset level，低于 minimum asset level 的 portfolio 不应该放进这个 composite 当中
2. 如有外汇差异
3. 如有对外国的投资
4. Treatment of withholding tax（FIRMS MUST disclose relevant details of the treatment of withholding taxes on dividends，interest income，and capital gains，if material）
5. 如有 leverage、derivatives、short position 的应用，要 disclose（FIRMS MUST disclose the presence，use，and extent of leverage，derivatives，and short positions，if material，including a description of the frequency of use and characteristics of the instruments sufficient to identify risks)；如果没用，可以不用 disclose
6. If the FIRM is redefined，the FIRM MUST disclose the date of，description of，and reason for the redefinition
7. If a COMPOSITE is redefined，the FIRM MUST disclose the date of，description of，and reason for the redefinition. Any change to a composite definition must not be applied retroactively

其他重要条款

0. Fundamental

✧ In cases in which laws and/or regulations conflict with the GIPS standards，firms are required to comply with the laws and regulations and make full disclosure of the conflict in the compliant presentation

✧ Firms must be defined as an investment firm，subsidiary，or division held out to clients or prospective clients as a distinct business entity

- 以一个独立的公司形象呈现在客户面前：独立做投资决策，独立运营，marketing 时要是一个独立的单位

✧ If the Firm does not meet all the requirements of the GIPS standards，the must not represent or state that it is " in compliance with the Global Investment Performance Standards except for…" or make any other statements that may indicate partial compliance with the GIPS standards

- 要遵守就要遵守全部条款，不能说"除了哪一条以外，其他都遵守"；也不能单独一个 composite 遵守，要全公司一起遵守

✧ Total firm asset (fair value)：Discretionary and non-discretionary assets，fee-paying and non-fee-paying portfolios

1. Input Data（主要是 portfolio value 作为输入数据）& 2.Calculation Methodology

✧ Value portfolio & return calculation (portfolio return and composite return)：At least monthly & the date of large cash flow

✧ Returns from cash and cash equivalents held in portfolios must be included in all return calculations

✧ Firms must calculate time-weighted rates of return (TWRR) that adjust for external cash flows. Both periodic and sub-period returns must be geometrically linked

3. Composite Construction

- ✧ Composite：Actual discretionary fee-paying portfolio must be included，discretionary non-fee-paying portfolio may be included，non-discretionary must not be included
  - 一旦 non-discretionary，就要立刻从 composite 当中移除出去
- ✧ 一个 portfolio 可以放在多个 composite 当中（Model/simulated portfolio 不能放在 composite 里面。Firms must not link performance of simulated or model portfolios with actual performance）
- ✧ Composite returns must be calculated by asset-weighting the individual portfolio returns using beginning-of-period values or a method that reflects both beginning-of-period values and external cash flows
- ✧ Composites must include new portfolios on a timely and consistent basis after each portfolio comes under management
- ✧ Terminated portfolios must be included in the historical performance of the composite up to the last full measurement period that each portfolio was under management
- ✧ For periods ≥ 2010，a carve-out must not be included in a composite unless the carve-out is managed separately with its own cash balance

5. Presentation and Reporting

- ✧ At least 5 years of performance (or since inception if less than five years) that meets the requirements of the GIPS standards. After a firm presents a minimum of five years of GIPS compliant performance，the firm must present an additional year of performance each year，building up to a minimum of 10 years of GIPS compliant performance
  - 宣称遵守 GIPS 那年要往前追溯 5 年的业绩按照 GIPS 标准来重新编撰（不足 5 年，自成立之日起），从宣称的那一年开始，每往后一年，就多一年的数据，一直增长到累积了 10 年数据之后就可以了，再增长一年可以把前面的数据给砍掉，保证数据库至少有 10 年业绩是按照 GIPS 标准的

GIPS Advertising Guidelines

✧ MUST disclose：

1. The definition of the firm
2. How a prospective client can obtain a compliant presentation and/or the firm's list of composite descriptions
3. The GIPS compliance statement for advertisements

✧ If present performance results， MUST also disclose：

4. The composite description
5. Composite total returns according to one of the following (Note： Returns for periods of less than one year MUST NOT be annualized)：
   - 1， 3， 5- annualized composite returns (or since the composite inception date)
   - Period-to-date composite returns + 1， 3， 5- annualized composite returns (or since...)
   - Period-to-date composite returns + 5 years of annual composite returns (or since...)
6. Performance is gross and/or net of fees
7. Total return for Benchmark
8. Benchmark description → If no benchmark， why
9. The currency for performance
10. The presence， use and extent of leverage， derivatives and short positions
11. Period of noncompliant performance before 2000
12. Laws and/or regulations conflict with GIPS

Valuation Hierarchy（估值层次）

1. Using objective，*observable*，unadjusted quoted *market prices* for identical investments in *active* markets
2. Objective，observable quoted *market prices for similar investments* in *active* markets
3. Quoted prices for identical or similar investments in markets that are *not active*
4. *Market-based inputs*，other than quoted prices，that are observable for the investment
5. *Subjective unobservable* inputs for the investment where markets are not active at the measurement date. Unobservable inputs SHOULD only be used to measure FAIR VALUE

CFA协会投资系列　CFA协会机构投资系列

机械工业出版社华章公司历时三年，陆续推出了《CFA协会投资系列》（共9本）《CFA协会机构投资系列》（共4本）两套丛书。这两套丛书互为补充，为读者提供了完整而权威的CFA知识体系（Candidate Body of Knowledge，简称CBOK），内容涵盖定量分析方法、宏微观经济学、财务报表分析方法、公司金融、估值与投资理论和方法、固定收益证券及其管理、投资组合管理、风险管理、投资组合绩效测评、财富管理等，同时覆盖CFA考试三个级别的内容，按照知识领域进行全面系统的介绍，是所有准备参加CFA考试的考生，所有金融专业院校师生的必读书。

序号	丛书名	中文书号	中文书名	原作者	定价
1	CFA协会投资系列	978-7-111-45367-3	公司金融：实用方法	Michelle R. Clayman,Martin S. Fridson,George H. Troughton	99
2	CFA协会投资系列	978-7-111-38805-0	股权资产估值（原书第2版）	Jeffrey K.Pinto,Elaine Henry,Jerald E. Pinto,Thomas R. Robinson,John D. Stowe,Abby Cohen	99
3	CFA协会投资系列	978-7-111-38802-9	定量投资分析（原书第2版）	Jerald E. Pinto, Richard A. DeFusco,Dennis W. McLeavey,David E. Runkle	99
4	CFA协会投资系列	978-7-111-38719-0	投资组合管理：动态过程（原书第3版）	John L. Maginn,Donald L. Tuttle,Dennis W. McLeavey,Jerald E. Pinto	149
5	CFA协会投资系列	978-7-111-50852-6	固定收益证券分析（原书第2版）	Frank J. Fabozzi	99
6	CFA协会投资系列	978-7-111-46112-8	国际财务报表分析	Thomas R. Robinson, Elaine Henry, Wendy L. Pirie, Michael A. Broihahn	149
7	CFA协会投资系列	978-7-111-50407-8	投资决策经济学：微观、宏观与国际经济学	Christopher D. Piros	99
8	CFA协会投资系列	978-7-111-46447-1	投资学：投资组合理论和证券分析	Michael G. McMillan	99
9	CFA协会投资系列	978-7-111-47542-2	新财富管理：理财顾问客户资产管理指南	Roger C. Gibson	99
10	CFA协会机构投资系列	978-7-111-43668-3	投资绩效测评：评估和结果呈报	Todd Jankowski,Watts S. Humphrey, James W. Over	99
11	CFA协会机构投资系列	2016即将出版	风险管理：变化的金融世界的基础	Austan Goolsbee,Steven Levitt,Chad Syverson	149
12	CFA协会机构投资系列	978-7-111-47928-4	估值技术：现金流贴现、收益质量、增加值衡量和实物期权	David T. Larrabee	99
13	CFA协会机构投资系列	978-7-111-49954-1	私人财富管理：财富管理实践	Stephen M. Horan	99

CFA协会金融前沿译丛

本套丛书为机械工业出版社华章公司与北京CFA协会携手合作，翻译、出版的一系列金融投资领域的前沿著作，甄选全球金融领域最新鲜、实用的金融知识和经验，务求贴合广大金融从业人员的实践需要。

书名	作者	ISBN	价格
华尔街证券分析	Jeffrey C. Hooke	9787111552048	79.00元
债券投资策略	Anthony Crescenzi	9787111524434	69.00元
REITs:人员、流程和管理	David Parker	9787111513544	59.00元
并购指南：如何发现好公司	Jeffrey C. Hooke	9787111520481	59.00元
证券化与结构化融资：全流程最佳实践指南	Markus Krebsz	9787111547679	99.00元
现金流建模边学边练	Keith A. Allman	9787111521211	49.00元
债券组合投资	Vineer Bhansali	9787111530152	59.00元
投资组合绩效测评实用方法	Carl R. Bacon	9787111487623	59.00元
多资产配置：投资实践进阶	Pranay Gupta	9787111565956	69.00元
并购套利：全球并购投资策略（原书第2版）	Thomas Kirchner	9787111581239	80.00元
波动率微笑：宽客大师教你建模	Emanuel Derman	2017即将出版	60.00元(暂定)

品职教育
PZACADEMY.COM
《CFA 一考而过系列》
扫码下载App
让学习更轻松，让坚持更容易，助有梦的金融人逐梦成真。
品职在线试听课，64小时免费任意听，听过便超越地球人。
4 CFA 经典题（待出版）
3 CFA FlashCard（待出版）
2 CFA 框架图
1 CFA 中文精讲